# Sight and Seeing:
## A World of Light and Color

# Sight *and* Seeing:

## *A World of Light and Color*

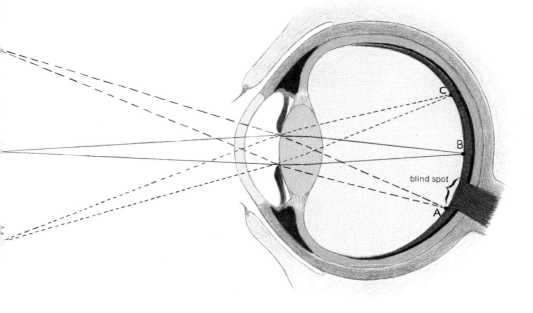

blind spot

## HILDA SIMON

## PHILOMEL BOOKS
### NEW YORK

Copyright © 1983 by Hilda Simon. All rights reserved.
First published in 1983 by Philomel Books,
a division of The Putnam Publishing Group,
51 Madison Avenue, New York, N.Y. 10010.
Printed in the United States of America.

Library of Congress Cataloging in Publication Data
Simon, Hilda. Sight and seeing.
Includes index.
Summary: Discusses the importance of the sense of sight,
the difference between sensitivity to light and the actual
formation of images, and the various sight organs found in animals.
1. Eye—Juvenile literature.   2. Vision—Juvenile
literature.   [1. Eye.   2. Vision]   I. Title.
QP475.7.S55   5976'.01823   82-3721
ISBN 0-399-20929-8

# Contents

# Seeing the Light:

## An Introduction

According to the familiar old saw, seeing is believing. Like many proverbs, it is a much too sweeping and generalized statement, for all of us believe things that we do not or cannot see. Yet this much is true: the act of seeing is indeed a central ingredient of human knowledge. In any unabridged dictionary, the listings under the verb *see* and its companion verb *look* are so numerous that they take up several columns. We see about, see fit, see the light, see to, look after, look into, look up to, and look out for, to name only a few. "I see" is the standard expression for denoting our understanding of a problem, an issue, or a viewpoint. The figurative use of *see* in this instance is based upon the undeniable fact that visual proof is often needed for a full and complete understanding: "one picture is worth a thousand words."

Comparing the dictionary entries under the four other senses to those for sight provides an excellent yardstick of their relative importance. Such a search would show that hearing ranks second, even though the listings for the verbs *hear* and *listen* are much shorter than those relating to sight. Touch and smell follow as numbers three and four, while taste runs a rather distant fifth. Clearly, then, the language test confirms the overwhelming importance of the sense of sight. This is borne out by all experience, for the ability to perceive objects dominates our life. Reading, writing, sewing, driving a car, cooking, watching TV, painting, making repairs, admiring a bed of colorful flowers, or observing birds at a feeder in wintertime—none of those activities would be possible without the ability to see. Yet we rarely think about it in such terms, for most people take vision as much for granted as they do breathing or sleeping. It is a very human trait to begin valuing the functions of our body only after something starts to go wrong with them. Blindness, whether it results from some biological accident, from injury, or from illness, involves a tragic malfunction or loss, either of the organ of sight itself or else of the all-important nerve connections to and within the optic centers of the brain. Great strides have been made in providing helpful devices so that the blind or near-blind can partake more fully in many areas of human endeavor. But none of these compensations can substitute for that seemingly simple yet wondrous ability to see.

The prerequisite for seeing is light: without light, there is no sight. Contrary to what many people believe, there is no creature that can see in total darkness, for seeing depends upon a certain amount of reflected light, no matter how small. The mere ability to distinguish between light and darkness, however, does not constitute sight as we understand it, for sight involves much more: the forming of images by an organ of vision. The difference between light and darkness, on the other hand, can be distinguished by organisms that have no visual organs of any kind, a fact of which green plants offer convincing proof. Everyone has seen indoor plants growing away from the darker areas of the room and towards the window or other light source. Green plants can "tell" light from darkness because they have special cells that are sensitive to light, without which they cannot live.

The reasons for the plants' dependence upon light can be found in the vital importance of *radiant energy*—the scientific term for light—to the internal mechanisms of all green vegetation. For instead of needing light to see by, as higher animals do, plants need it to produce their own food. The importance of this process cannot be overestimated, for as plants produce the food they need, they also provide the basis for all other life on earth. With chlorophyll, the green coloring matter in plants, acting as the agent, the plant can use light to fundamentally alter certain chemical compounds in its environment; this process is known as photosynthesis, which might be translated as "light-mixing." Although light in the form of radiant energy is unable to sustain life, the plant has the unique ability to convert it into all-important chemical energy. Light acted upon by chlorophyll transforms two inorganic compounds, water and carbon dioxide, into organic compounds, and the simple sugars so formed provide the basis for more complex substances including starch, oil, cellulose, and double sugars. That in itself is marvelous because all these substances are chemically unstable, whereas the inorganic molecules from which they are made up, if left to themselves, have a tendency toward the chemical stability that is the hallmark of lifeless matter.

Apart from its indirect importance through photosynthesis, radiant energy also performs vital, direct roles both as heat, without which animal life would not be possible, and as light, which permits all those animals equipped with efficient eyes to see their environment. The ability to form visual images of their surroundings gives higher animals the freedom to engage in activities and adopt ways of life which are denied forever to those creatures having no eyes at all or else very weak and inefficient visual organs. Some sight-related activities among the higher vertebrates go far beyond those necessary to sustain life and ensure reproduction—they actually impart a heightened sense of well-being. For human beings, the "nonvital" fields of endeavor, such as art, poetry, and music, are in fact an essential part of cultural and spiritual self-expression.

In this context, it is well to remember that the elementary activities of life—eating, sleeping, mating, reproducing—can, and as a matter of fact often do, take place in darkness, and therefore do not require organs of sight. Animals that have no eyes manage to eat and sleep and mate and reproduce without any difficulty; even among highly organized animals, many of these activities typically take place under cover of night. By contrast, among creatures that have the organs necessary to convert light waves into images and vibrational energy into sounds, any activity that goes beyond the fulfillment of the basic, primitive needs to sustain life and ensure reproduction *has* to take place in a world of light—and usually of sound also. Inquisitiveness, a trait found in many higher animals and a vital ingredient of our own intellectual progress, rests almost entirely upon the ability to examine objects visually.

In the human context, the areas of art and science offer the most striking illustrations of the extent to which "higher" activities are based upon the ability to transform reflected light into images. Painting, sculpture, and architecture, among others, depend upon that ability both for creating and appreciating such works of art.

Unlike sight and hearing—and to a much lesser extent touch—smell and taste play little or no role in artistic creations, nor do they have an important part in advancing scientific research, which depends almost entirely upon the ability to observe and compare visually. The microscope and the telescope, both of which enhance and increase our visual capacity, are used with good reason as common symbols of science.

But modern research has established the fact that light entering through the eyes serves many important functions beyond those connected with sight. The field of photobiology supplies clues to a number of health-related questions,

The snail's eye on the left and the ocellus on the right both have the basic components of a simple image-forming organ.

for scientists are finding increasing evidence that full-spectrum, or normal daylight, has profound and beneficial effects on the body chemistry. Unfortunately, even window glass shuts out some of the wavelengths, and most artificial light is reduced-spectrum light. This is especially true of the "cool white" fluorescent light, which concentrates on the yellow-green parts of the spectrum and contains almost no longwave ultraviolet. Yet it is precisely the full-spectrum light absorbed through the eyes that influences vital endocrine functions, thereby affecting resistance to colds and infections, absorption of calcium by the intestines, and sexual development. There is also considerable evidence that reduced-spectrum light promotes the rate of tumor growth, so that we may find that further research in this area will provide important clues to cancer control. Many hospitals are already using phototherapy to treat certain illnesses, and especially the jaundiced condition dangerous to many premature babies. And an experiment in Florida showed a dramatic decrease in hyperactivity among children when fluorescent lights were replaced by full-spectrum lighting.

Against this background of what the gift of sight means to us, any examination of the various visual organs found in the animal world takes on a special meaning. The miracle and mystery of vision and the mind-boggling complexity of its apparatus are impressive indeed. The high degree of visual development in some animal groups presents a striking contrast to the total lack of any organ of sight in others. A closer examination quickly reveals that an astonishingly large percentage of the animal kingdom consists of sightless creatures. Beginning with the one-celled animals, it ranges

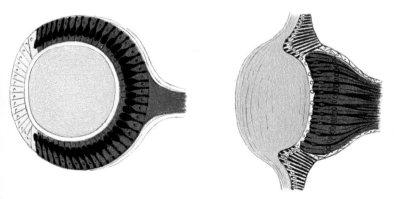

all the way through the nine large and several small primary divisions that rank below the insects and their kin. Only a relative handful of the tens of thousands of species that make up these groups have eyes capable of forming clear images, although many possess light-sensitive but nonvisual *eyespots*. Such eyespots are a means of distinguishing light from darkness and may be located in different parts of the body—at the tips of the starfish's tentacles, along the mantle margin of the jellyfish, or scattered all over the earthworm's body. Such light-sensitive cells may have a function that differs greatly from those normally associated with eyes. In earthworms, for instance, they serve to warn their owners *away* from the light, which explains why worms coming up to the surface at night will try to get back underground as fast as possible when they are exposed to a sudden light. They cannot, however, detect red light; fishermen often use red-shaded lanterns when they go out at night to collect earthworms for bait.

Mollusks are the only animal group below the arthropod level among which functional eyes do occur, although many mollusks, such as clams and scallops, do not have organs of sight. At the other extreme, the eyes of squids and octopuses are so highly developed that they rival those of vertebrate animals. Many snails, on the other hand, can probably do little more than distinguish between light and dark shapes, although some—predatory snails especially—have better vision. The typical snail eye is very simply structured but has a protective cornea covering the lens and a pigmented background, or retina, containing light-sensitive cells connected to a nerve.

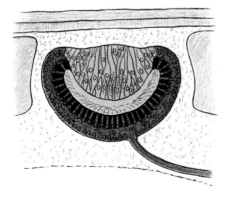

Located well beneath the skin, the pineal eye appears to be the remnant of a once-important sense organ. The lenslike structure is colored blue, the light-sensitive area and the connecting nerve, red, and the vitreous body, light green.

Another type of simple eye is the *ocellus,* which is Latin and means "little eye." These "eyelets" occur in numerous immature insect forms such as the larvae of beetles and in most adult insects in addition to the larger, multifaceted *compound eyes.* An ocellus is probably capable of forming crude images but is not at all efficient.

The list of organs sensitive to changes in light intensity would not be complete without the most peculiar and puzzling of all "eyes," the so-called third eye, known to scientists as the *pineal eye.* Located beneath the skin at the top of the head in a space between two bones covering the roof of the skull, this curious structure is found in many reptiles and amphibians. Covered by a more or less translucent scale or membrane, and possessing vestiges of a lens as well as a pigmented, light-sensitive background, the pineal eye looks remarkably like some of the eyespots of invertebrate animals. Although its sensitivity to light has been proven in tests with lizards, its function is unknown; scientists believe it to be the residue of a once-important organ.

Any review of the rudimentary and simple eyes of lower animals serves to highlight the fact that, with the sole exception of squids and octopuses, really efficient eyes are confined to just two groups: the arthropods, meaning the insects and their relatives, and the vertebrates ranging from fish to mammals. A closer look at the image-forming eyes yields fascinating insights into the complexities and refinements, many of them still not fully understood, that permit the miracle of vision to occur in so many different animals. That miracle is rendered even more tantalizing by the mystery surrounding the origin of the sense organs which make it possible for us to live in a world of light and color.

# Mosaic Images

The fossil record—impressions and traces of living things preserved in the earth's crust—stretches back some 500 million years, beginning rather abruptly in what is known as the Cambrian period. Scientists believe that the virtual absence of fossils before that time is due to the fact that the creatures living then were all soft-bodied and therefore left no impression in the sediment of those primeval oceans. That theory, however, does not explain the sudden appearance of so many hard-shelled animals without the transitional stages presumed to be necessary for the development of any distinct group. Even more astonishing is the fact that those Cambrian animals were complex rather than primitive organisms, and that many of the basic divisions of the animal kingdom are represented among them.

The fossils of Cambrian arthropods called trilobites offer some very clear evidence of rather advanced features. Trilobites were shrimplike creatures with an oval, segmented body and many small legs. More important, however, is the fact that they had a distinct head equipped with a pair of slender feelers and, usually, two relatively large, multifaceted eyes. We are certain of that because the hard outer shell of dead trilobites permitted the preservation of detailed impressions of their body outlines, including the eyes, in the ocean sediment which later hardened into fossilized rock. On the basis of what is currently known, there is no reason to believe that the eyes of the long-extinct Cambrian arthropods differed in any important way from those of modern species. That makes the compound eye the oldest known model of visual organ on earth; after remaining essentially unchanged for half a billion years, it apparently still is as satisfactory for the modern arthropods as it was for their ancient forebears.

Almost everyone knows that insects have compound eyes made up of many tiny individual units, but very few people really understand how such eyes function, or why some are more efficient than others without being basically different. Because their structure is quite unlike that of the vertebrate eye, the insect's eyes look strangely expressionless to us, being not only immovably fixed in their position, but also lacking such features as iris, pupil, and eyelids. At least, however, they are located in the familiar position at either side of the head. Insect bodies function in strange ways, and their sensory organs are often located at equally strange sites, at least from our point of view. In addition to breathing through holes in the side of the body, insects smell—and also frequently hear—with their feelers. On the other hand, many insect musicians such as crickets and long-horned grasshoppers, including katydids, have "ears" in their elbows, meaning that the first joint of each foreleg is equipped with a sound-sensitive membrane. And then there are the butterflies that taste substances by stepping in them; they "put their foot in it" all the time. Taste buds in their feet tell them whether or not they have stepped into something that promises a sweet meal and is worth the trouble of unrolling their long tongue.

Considering such radical departures from what we are used to thinking of as the "right" place for sense organs, it seems almost surprising that the insect's eyes are in fact located where we would expect them to be. That location, however, only serves to underline the special nature of all eyes as image-forming organs requiring an unobstructed field of vision. Hearing with one's elbows and tasting with one's feet may be quite feasible, but for organs of sight a very special location is needed. It could conceivably be argued that a head is required primarily as a site for the eyes, and indeed lower animals without eyes are typically distinguished by a conspicuous lack of any distinct head.

Although many crustaceans and adult insects have a few eyelets, or ocelli, their main visual organs are the large, paired compound eyes. Those of crabs and lobsters are typically located atop movable stalks that can be swiveled about to look in different directions. The eyes of most insects, on the other hand, do not stand out from the head and cannot be rotated or otherwise moved. Since many insects such as beetles are unable to turn their head, it would seem that they have a very limited field of vision. That, however, is not entirely true because the compound eyes' special structure allows insects—particularly those with the larger eyes—to look in several directions at the same time.

All compound eyes have a similar basic design; the typi-

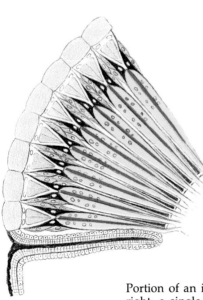

*Color Code*

Cornea-lens: green
Crystalline cone: blue
Pigment: black/gray
Retinal rod: red
Sensory cells: yellow

Portion of an insect's eye. On the right, a single, greatly enlarged ommatidium reveals its component structures.

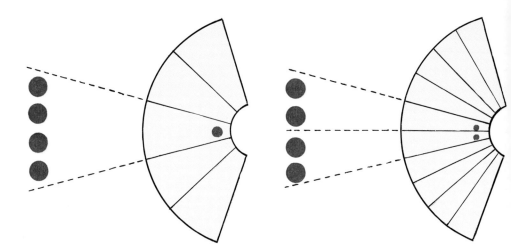

cal eye is round or oval and strongly convex, with a surface divided up into many tiny sections. Under a microscope, these sections appear as exquisitely symmetrical six-sided facets joined together like the cells of a honeycomb, often colored with beautiful iridescent hues. Each of the facets serves as a combination of protective covering and lens for a slender, pencil-shaped structure known as an *ommatidium*, from the Greek word *omma* for eye. Far from being just a portion of the whole eye, each ommatidium is a self-contained visual unit, a tiny eyelet complete with its own individual image-forming apparatus. It consists of the hard corneal outer lens, a crystalline cone serving as an enhancement of the lens and located directly beneath, and a long, tapering structure called the *retinula*. Made up of eight sensory cells whose center forms the retinal rod, its pointed end leads into the optic nerve. A mantle of dark pigment surrounds all or part of each ommatidium like a tight-fitting sleeve and screens it off from neighboring units. The extent of that pigment screen is the one important difference between two otherwise similar types of compound eyes. In those whose pigment sleeves are complete, all incoming light except that forming a straight line with the axis of the cone is absorbed, which means that only a relatively small

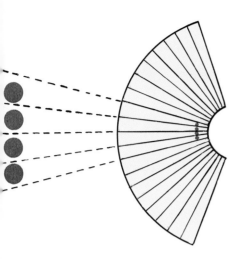

Graphic demonstration of the relationship between visual acuity of a compound eye and the number of ommatidia: as the number increases, more detail is recorded.

amount of light reaches the retinal rod. It also means that the visual impression of each ommatidium is separated from those of all others.

For insects with nocturnal habits, which have to be active in very dim light, the loss of so much incoming light through absorption by the pigment would result in virtual blindness. Such insects have a type of compound eye whose pigment sleeves are incomplete so that light which otherwise would be absorbed can enter neighboring ommatidia and be registered by their retinulas. Whatever the resulting image may lose in sharpness, it gains in light efficiency. For insects such as moths, which usually fly at dusk, that means they still can see where they are going. Some compound eyes are versatile, being able to adjust the amount of pigment as conditions vary. In bright light, the pigment sleeves are complete, but in weak light, they get smaller and so permit incoming light to cross over to neighboring ommatidia.

Because they are bunched together with their broad ends facing outward and their slender tips ending in the optic nerve, no two of the compound eye's tapering units point in exactly the same direction. This means that incoming light stimuli are different for each of the ommatidia of a

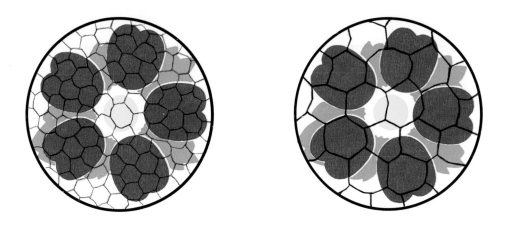

In any mosaic picture, a greater number of
pieces results in a clearer definition of shape.

typical compound eye such as that of the honeybee, whose
individual units have complete pigment sleeves. In effect,
therefore, the image in the bee's eye is made up of thousands of separate light impressions. One might compare
this to a mosaic picture put together from many tiny stones
or to the photomechanical "screen" made up of tiny dots
that is used to reproduce photographic images on paper.

The examples of both the mosaic picture and the printer's
screen provide good illustrations of why certain compound
eyes are keener and capable of registering more detail than
others. In any mosaic, detail is determined by the number
of stones or other individual units used for a given area of
the picture; the greater the number, the finer the detail. The
same holds true for the dots of the printer's screen; one
reason why newspaper pictures lack sharpness and often
look fuzzy is the relatively large size of the dots.

In the compound eye, the ommatidia take the place of the
mosaic stones or the screen dots: twice as many ommatidia
for a given area means an image that has twice as much
detail. Simply by counting the number of individual facets,
one can get a fair idea of any compound eye's power of
acuity. The eye of a crayfish, for instance, has some 2,500

ommatidia; although that may sound like a lot, a honeybee's eye has 6,500 units, and for some insects the number may range as high as 30,000! At the other end of the scale, there are those insects whose lives are dominated by their sense of smell, and whose eyes are small and not very important to their way of life. These include such species as roaches, many true bugs (those in the order Hemiptera), and numerous beetles, some of which may have eyes numbering only a few hundred units.

Even insects with large compound eyes, however, do not have anything approaching what we consider to be really keen vision. Compound eyes are efficient for registering movement, and many are equipped to perceive special light intensities and vibrations, but their capacity for forming sharply detailed images is very poor compared to that of the human eye. We know this because visual acuity is determined by the minimum angle required to visually separate two points. For a human eye, the angle at which two points still appear as separate impressions may be as little as one-sixtieth of a degree, compared to one full degree for the fairly keen compound eye of the honeybee. Human vision therefore is at least eighty times more acute than that of the average insect.

Photographs taken through the actual lens structure of compound eyes have confirmed that conclusion; images are fuzzy and lack sharp detail. Further proof of the compound eye's inferiority as an image-forming organ resulted from a

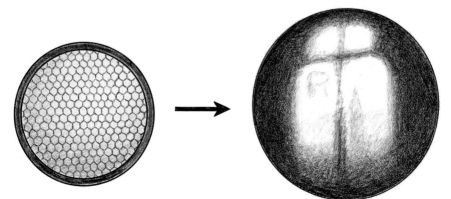

This photograph of a window and a church steeple beyond was made by using a glowworm's eye as a lens: a capital letter "R" had been pasted on one of the panes.

series of experiments designed to yield specific information about the vision of honeybees. These tests were part of a larger study of the honeybees' life by noted German biologist Dr. Karl von Frisch, who became famous through his book *The Dancing Bees*.

Any test attempting to discover the extent to which bees can form visual images—and therefore distinguish shapes—had to begin by training the bees to associate certain shapes with food sources, and then to find out whether they could distinguish those shapes from others. The results were quite surprising, for it turned out that widely differing solid shapes, including circles, squares, triangles, and rectangles, were consistently confused by the bees. Such apparent lack of discriminatory ability also applied to different outline figures, as well as to those that were branched or star-shaped. Bees proved unable, for instance, to distinguish between a cross and a square made of four dark lines enclosing a light space! But the moment any solid shape was alternated with one made up of light and dark lines and spaces, all confusion ended; the bees could tell them apart every time. It seemed clear on the basis of those tests that their powers of linear discrimination are determined not so much by the shape as we see it, but rather by the extent to which any figure is broken up into separate and contrasting elements. Well adapted to perceiving a rapid succession of objects or movements while in flight, and particularly sensitive to rich patterns of light and color, a bee's eye is much less geared to delineating the shapes of immobile objects, which to them are less important anyway.

On the other hand, they have a visual ability which is essential to them and which humans lack: they can distinguish polarized light. What this means is that bees have nothing less than a sensitive, built-in sky compass which helps them navigate during their nectar-seeking flights. It was Dr. von Frisch's observation that worker bees which

The four shapes in each of the two vertical rows look alike to honeybees, but they can recognize any shape in either row as different from any shape in the other. Similarly, they can distinguish the three shapes in the horizontal bottom row.

had been marked for identification returned from a distant nectar source in the afternoon and unhesitatingly headed for that same source the next morning, which led him to wonder how they did it. Scientists already knew that bees, like many arthropods, can distinguish polarized light. In the bee's eye, the eight sensory cells of each retinula act as a polarizing filter. These filters, it turns out, enable the bees to use not just the sun, but indeed the entire sky, as aids in their navigation.

Polarized light differs from ordinary light, which vibrates in all directions at once, in that its vibrations have a definite form and occur only on one plane, so that the beam resembles a flat ribbon rather than a round rope. According to whether it vibrates in circles, ovals, or straight lines, it is known as circularly, elliptically, or plane-polarized light. Artificial polarizers such as certain crystals are used in photography and other fields to polarize ordinary light by forcing its vibrations into a single plane. Polarized light is used widely in science with the help of such instruments as the polariscope. A variety of chemically identical substances, for instance, can now be examined and their organic or synthetic origins determined because molecules produced by living things are optically active, rotating and passing through a beam of polarized light. The synthetic molecule, however, is optically inactive and shuts out the light.

Sunlight contains both kinds; most light reflected from such surfaces as water, wet streets, or mirrors is polarized. So is much of the light coming from a blue sky on a sunny day, for the tiny water droplets and other particles suspended in the air have the tendency to bend and scatter light—especially plane-polarized blue light. Both the intensity and the direction of polarized-light vibrations vary with the position of the sun in the sky—in other words, with the time of the day. Because of their thousands of tiny polarizing filters pointing in different directions, bees know by

these light variations in which direction they are flying. They know this even when they cannot see the sun itself; a patch of blue sky is sufficient to give them their bearings. On heavily overcast days, however, their internal compass no longer works well and they can become disoriented, which is one reason why bees are usually about on clear, sunny days.

To find out how the bees' internal compass works, Dr. von Frisch and his researchers used an artificial polarizing filter which more or less duplicated that of the insects' retinula. The eight-sided, star-shaped filter was mounted on a table so that it could be adjusted for different directions and tilted towards the sky, which was then photographed through the filter at various times of the day. The results were striking, for the photographs showed different patterns for each time of the day as well as for each compass direction. It became clear that a bee flying south, for example, could not possibly stray southeast or southwest without noticing the significant change in light patterns.

Taken together, the research into the secret of bee navigation and orientation added up to astonishing revelations about these little insects. Not only are they optically tied to the sun and the sky: they also have an internal clock and a computer capable of utilizing complex optical information. Hardly less astonishing is that they can memorize the various light patterns for the different times of the day. It is this remarkable ability that enables a bee that has located a good nectar source one afternoon to find it again promptly early the next morning.

The large eyes of the worker bee are obviously necessary

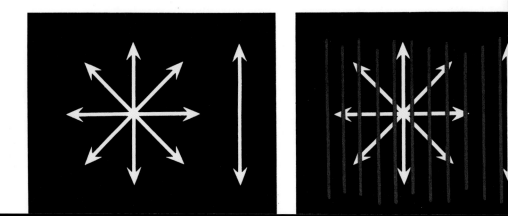

On the left, a transverse cut through an ommatidium of a bee's eye reveals its eight polarizing cells. In the vertical row on the right, photographs of the sky taken through an artificial eight-sided polarizing filter in four different compass directions reproduce the bee's internal "sky compass."

NORTH

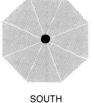

SOUTH

EAST

WEST

for the successful completion of her many chores, especially on flights outside the hive. The much larger eyes of the male bee, or drone, however, do not seem warranted by anything in its lifestyle. Drones never collect honey or pollen and never work around the hive either. In the words of noted German poet-humorist Wilhelm Busch, they are "lazy, stupid, fat, and greedy," and do nothing but loaf around and eat. Yet their eyes have fully twice as many units as those of the worker bees, which would be difficult to understand were it not that the sole reason for the drones' existence is found in their role as potential mates for the queen during her one and only nuptial flight. When the queen gets ready to mate, she leaves the hive on a bright sunny day, rises up into the air, and quickly disappears in a steep upward spiral flight. All the drones in the hive follow in hot pursuit, but only the swiftest and strongest among them has a chance to catch up and mate with the queen. To do that, however, he must keep her in sight during that dizzying flight, and therefore his eyes must be keen enough to detect that tiny, fast-moving speck in the sky.

Along with the need to elude their numerous enemies, finding a mate also seems to be one of the main reasons for the good vision of many flies, which otherwise—and especially when it comes to locating food—are guided by their exceedingly keen sense of smell. Anyone who has ever observed the speed with which flies manage to find any bit of rotting organic matter will agree that their nose is phenomenally keen, even if their choice of odors may seem deplorable to us. Along with that highly developed sense of smell, however, the advanced species including the so-

On the left, ordinary and plane-polarized light are shown side by side. On the right, polarizing material has been used to shut out all vibrations of ordinary light except those operating on one plane, thereby making the light plane-polarized.

called filth flies also have large and efficient eyes, some of which may number up to 18,000 units. (The word "advanced" in this context refers to the flies' anatomical structures and not necessarily to their habits!) It is small wonder, then, that trying to sneak up on and swat a housefly or bluebottle can be such a frustrating experience; these insects quite literally have eyes in the back of their head and are especially good at detecting movement, even if it comes from above or behind.

Regardless of how keen their vision may be, however, most insects, including bees and flies, still have to rely heavily on their sense of smell, which they may use for almost anything from locating food sources to identifying home territories or courting a mate. The exception to this rule is the group comprising the dragonflies and damselflies. One look at their huge, bulging eyes and their ridiculously small antennae tells us that these insects are quite obviously guided by their vision alone, and experiments have confirmed it. Often overspreading the head and meeting in the center in what is known as an *eyeseam*, a dragonfly's eyes may have as many as 30,000 individual units each. The head of the familiar green darner, for example, appears to consist of nothing more than eyes and mouth. Because the eyes command such a very large field

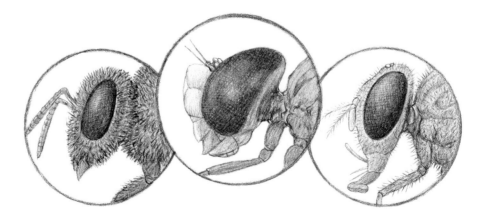

The head of a bee, a dragonfly, and a fly
reveal the comparative size and
prominence of the eyes.

of vision, it is very difficult to approach, let alone capture, a resting dragonfly.

Like all compound eyes, those of dragonflies are very efficient for detecting movement. In addition, however, these insects have a pronounced ability to judge distances correctly as they zero in on their flying prey during their swift, darting hunting forays. Because so large a portion of the eyes faces forward, their binocular vision is good, meaning they can see an object with both eyes and therefore from two slightly differing angles, which provides the "range finder" necessary for estimating distances and striking their prey with accuracy. Such accuracy could not be achieved with monocular vision because the pinpointing angle would be missing. Although they lack any mechanism for focus adjustments, dragonflies are relatively farsighted and capable of detecting movement at more than ten yards away.

Close observation of immature dragonflies has yielded a great deal of information about the extent to which these insects have to rely on their eyes for capturing food. Because dragonflies are primitive insects, they undergo a gradual development rather than the complete metamorphosis of higher insects such as flies, whose immature stages include a wormlike, often legless and eyeless larva and an immobile pupa. Before anyone concludes too hastily that being primitive is a drawback for an insect, let it be said that dragonflies, both in their immature and their adult stages, capture and eat large numbers of both larval and mature advanced insects. Because pest species such as houseflies and mosquitoes are high on the dragonflies' shopping list of desirable tidbits, we can only be grateful for their voracious appetites. In fact, adult dragonflies pursue mosquitoes so relentlessly that they have earned the nickname of "mosquito hawks."

The immature stage of dragonflies is called a nymph; it is a peculiar-looking aquatic creature which lives and hunts in the water of pools, ponds, and brooks. Nymphs will eat any small aquatic animal they can overpower; in many stagnant pools, much of their diet consists of mosquito larvae.

The nymphs have a segmented body, six legs, compound eyes, and a peculiar apparatus consisting of a greatly elongated lower lip or *labium*. It forms a kind of extendable grasping tongs which normally lies folded beneath the head, covering part of the face like a mask. Whenever a suitable prey moves into striking distance, the lip is shot forward with lightning speed and deadly accuracy.

Intrigued by the seemingly infallible aim of captive green darner nymphs, one biologist decided to find out whether their hunting success was entirely a matter of keen binocular vision, or whether the nymphs perhaps supplemented it by smell or touch. After covering the eyes of half a dozen nymphs with black paint, he released them into an aquarium stocked with mosquito larvae. The result left no further doubt: not a single one of the "blindfolded" nymphs was able to capture any prey, and they all would have starved had they remained in that condition.

As his next experiment, this observer covered only one of each of the nymphs' eyes with black paint. Although they now could see their prey, and desperately tried to aim for it, they always struck either too far left or too far right, depending upon which eye was covered. Those misses were clear proof that they needed binocular vision for accuracy in judging distances; with only one eye, their range finder was unable to function properly. The most fascinating development in that experiment, however, came after a few days when two of the seven one-eyed nymphs proved that, even on the invertebrate level, individuals of the same species and from the same batch of eggs may have unequal learning capabilities. After many frustrating misses, the two "smart" nymphs learned to overcome their handicap by creeping up sideways on their prey in a crablike fashion and then aiming slightly to one side. That maneuver netted them a mosquito larva almost every time. Evidently each of the nymph's large eyes has some crude binocular vision which may be used in this way—*if* the individual chooses to learn it, for it is clearly not an instinctive, inherited part of the dragonflies' genetic makeup.

The fact that smell and touch have practically no part at all in the dragonfly's life has been confirmed by removing the insects' tiny antennae; they hardly seem to notice the loss, nor does it hinder them in any of their normal activities. It is the dragonfly's superior vision alone that helps it to find and capture its prey, court its mate, distinguish and guard against rival males, and escape from enemies. Even the female's selection of a suitable place to deposit her eggs is made on a purely visual basis, which occasionally may lead her to mistake the shimmering surface of wet paved streets for that of a body of water.

Dragonflies would deserve our gratitude and admiration if only because of their role as predators of so many insect pests. But there is more to our feeling for dragonflies; along with bees and colorful butterflies, these are the graceful insects about which poets often write, and which artists love to depict. To the English poet Tennyson, a dragonfly was a "living flash of light;" to the Japanese, it is the symbol of victory, and Oriental artists for centuries have cast it in silver or bronze, or pictured it in delicate drawings on china or silk. Perhaps the reason for such admiration may be found at least partly in the fact that we, too, are visual creatures, and therefore cannot help feeling a certain kinship with insects whose eyes are their life as they wing their way under a sunny sky on a summer's day.

# *Seeing Our Way*

Although the multifaceted, compound-type of visual organ is found in the greatest number of animal species, it remains confined to the invertebrate level. Drawbacks of the compound eye include its rigidly fixed position, lack of any mechanism for focus change, and limited degree of visual acuity. The wide range of often highly specialized ways of life typical of the backboned, higher animals was possible only with the aid of appropriate organs of sight. As for the human race, there is no conceivable way in which civilization and historical development could have occurred without the full range and refinement of human vision.

The "camera-type" eye is common to all vertebrates from fish to mammals, but its origin remains a mystery. A multitude of intricate, interrelated structural details and nerve connections make the vertebrates' visual apparatus the most complex of all sensory organs. So far, no one has been able to offer any satisfactory theory on how it might have evolved; attempts at tracing its evolution through the study of the individual phases of eye formation in vertebrate embryos have not been successful.

A rudimentary vertebrate eye representing an in-between stage does not exist. Although scientists believe that *Amphioxus*, the lancelet, is an intermediate form between the invertebrate and vertebrate groups, this curious fishlike, transparent creature has no hint of true eye structure. The lancelet does have many single light-sensitive cells grouped in the marrow of its spinal chord, but none of those cells show any trace of image-forming structures.

On the other hand, fully developed eyes are present in the lamprey, the most primitive living backboned animal, and one which lacks many of the vertebrate's other typical features. Despite a superficial resemblance to eels, lampreys are not true fishes, having no defined head, no jaws, and only a single nasal opening. Some of them are parasitic; attaching themselves to fishes with their disk-shaped mouths, they use their many sharp rasping teeth to bore a hole into their victim's body and drain its blood. Infestations of the Great Lakes with lampreys some decades ago all but destroyed the local game fish populations before they were brought under control. Interesting to scientists as living links to the earliest known backboned animals, lampreys are a peculiar mixture of primitive body structures and such advanced features as the higher animals' lateral pair of eyes.

In our technological age, the image-forming mechanism of the vertebrate eye is often explained in terms of the photographic camera. That comparison is helpful in illustrating some optical facts and functions of vision, yet even the finest camera is no more than an approximation of just one portion of the visual apparatus. The real miracle of sight begins at the point where all comparison with the camera ends.

Even though the basic design is similar for all vertebrate eyes, a variety of modifying features make it possible for individual animal groups to have special capabilities such as extreme far-sightedness, dim-light acuity, and good underwater vision. Each of these modifications of the basic design is useful for a specific way of life and provides fascinating insights into the means by which such adaptations have been achieved.

Although it differs in many details from those of other vertebrates, the human eye can serve as a general "type model," especially of mammalian visual organs. Extensive research into human vision has provided a great deal of detailed information about its anatomy and functions, and much of that applies to all vertebrate eyes.

Compared to other sense organs such as the nose or ears, the eyes are clearly different in that their external, visible parts are more delicate but also more elaborately equipped against injury. Lying beneath bony ridges, they are protected by movable lids which completely cover them during sleep; a fringe of eyelashes helps to guard them during waking hours.

The necessary lubrication of the outer eye surface is supplied by the various glands that ring the eye. Some of these glands secrete the salty—and therefore mildly antiseptic—fluid that washes constantly over the exposed part of the eye and is known as tears when produced in excess. The tear fluid has an extremely important role in keeping the eye healthy, and the inability to secrete enough of this fluid to ensure sufficient moistening of its surface is a serious ailment. Human eyes and those of many mammals have several tear glands each, with ducts leading to the inner rim of the eyelids, which are lined with mucous membranes and have glands of their own. Whenever a foreign body such as a tiny particle of soot or grime lodges in the eye, these glands produce a soft mucous coating that envelops the for-

Glands that lubricate the mammalian eye. Tear glands and ducts are colored blue, lid glands, green, and the remnant of the nictitating membrane, yellow.

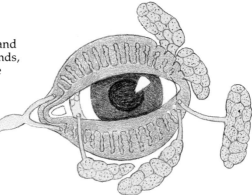

eign matter and lessens the irritation. Unless it is too deeply embedded or aggravated by rubbing, it will then usually be washed away from the sensitive areas and into the corner of the eye by the tear fluid. This elaborate safety system of glands serves to accentuate the unique nature of the eye as the most delicate—and probably the most vulnerable—of all sensory organs.

The light-sensitive structures of the eye are located deep inside the eyeball, which lies in the hollow, or orbit, beneath the eyelids, and is cushioned by layers of fat. The eyeball can be rotated by muscles attached to both sides, so that the eyes can be moved to look upward, sideways, and downward even while the head and body may remain motionless. The outer covering of the eyeball forms a supporting case consisting of tough, hard connective tissue; this is called the *sclera*, also referred to as the *scleroid* coat. In the exposed front part of the eye, the tissue is transparent and becomes the *cornea*. An inner lining for the scleroid coat is provided by the *choroid*, or membranous, coat, which contains not only the necessary blood vessels but also the large amount of dark pigment needed to exclude all light except that entering from the front.

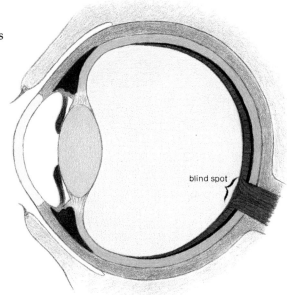

Structure of the human eye, which in its basic components is similar to all other vertebrate eyes.

*Color Code*

Cornea: yellow
Lens: blue
Iris: brown
Ligaments: tan
Ciliary muscles: purple
Choroid coat: green
Sclera: orange
Aqueous humor: white
Vitreous humor: blue-green
Retina/optic nerve: red
Pigment: black

blind spot

Focus change in the mammalian eye. The top half shows the lens in its normal, rather convex shape. In the bottom half, relaxation of the ciliary muscle has tightened the ligaments and thereby flattened the lens for distant viewing.

*Color Code*

Cornea: yellow
Lens: blue
Iris: brown
Ligaments: tan
Ciliary muscles: purple
Choroid coat: green
Sclera: orange

The foremost portion of the choroid coat is specialized into the circular *iris,* whose pigmentation lends the distinctive coloration to the eye. All shades of brown, from light hazel to almost black, are produced by the same dark pigment known as melanin. Blue eyes, on the other hand, are not the result of pigmentation. In humans, blue eyes are found only among the white race, but they do occur in some animals; the Siamese cat is only one example. That blue is a non-pigmental, non-chemical color caused by submicroscopic tissue structures which selectively reflect certain light waves.

Located in the center of the iris is the *pupil,* a circular opening corresponding to the lens aperture in the front of the camera. (Some nocturnal animals have an elliptical pupil: they are "cat-eyed.") The pupil contracts or expands to regulate the amount of light entering the eye and striking the transparent, convex *lens,* which is suspended by special ligaments directly behind the pupil. In both its shape and optical properties, the organic lens of the eye resembles the glass lens of the camera.

The focusing mechanism of human as well as most other vertebrate eyes differs from that of the camera in that the camera lens is moved back and forth to accommodate near and distant objects. However, focus is achieved in the mammalian eye by changes in the curvature of the lens itself: special muscles acting upon the ligaments by which the lens is suspended change the degree of convexity. The lens is flattened for more distant focusing and returns to its more strongly curved shape for closeup viewing.

The space between the cornea and the lens is filled with a watery substance called the *aqueous humor*, which is a mouthful but means, quite simply, "watery fluid." The larger space behind the lens is taken up by a clear, colorless but somewhat thicker and more jellylike mass known as the *vitreous humor*, or "glassy fluid." These substances serve the dual purpose of maintaining the shape of the eyeball and keeping the lens and other parts well lubricated.

With the lens suspended between two more or less fluid substances, the light entering through the pupil must pass through four different media—cornea, aqueous humor, lens, and vitreous humor—before reaching the back wall. So clear and delicately adjusted to the properties of light are these various substances that the light suffers almost no distortion or loss of intensity by the time it arrives at the innermost layer of the choroid coat, or *retina*.

The retina, which corresponds to the film in our camera example, consists of tens of millions of light-sensitive receptor cells, which come in two different shapes: long, slender *rods*, and shorter, stouter *cones*. The rods number about 115 million in the human eye and are efficient for forming colorless images in dim light with the help of a protein pigment called rhodopsin by scientists, but popularly known as "visual purple." Bright light bleaches this purple pigment from the rods, which explains why people are temporarily blinded and unable to see anything when they pass abruptly from a very brightly lit to a very dimly lit area. As the visual purple in the rods is replaced, vision in reduced light returns.

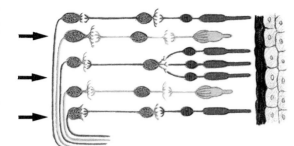

Portion of the retinal area of a vertebrate's inverse eye. All the rods and cones point backward; arrows indicate the direction of incoming light. On the right, a single rod and cone, greatly magnified. Rods, red; cones, yellow; nerve cells, orange.

The cones function in exactly the opposite way, meaning that they are active in bright light, responding to both the composite so-called white light—which in reality is colorless—and to specific wavelengths of that light which we see as colors. It is the presence of cones in our eyes that has a direct bearing on our ability to see color. The normal human eye has about 6.5 million cones; they are most numerous in a small, sensitive spot in the retina called the *fovea*, which is the area of greatest visual acuity.

Many mammals, and particularly those with nocturnal habits including cats and other carnivores, have in the retinal area a membranous layer known to biologists as the *tapetum lucidum*, which literally translated from Latin means "shining carpet." It is made up of fibrous or platelike cells that reflect source light, thereby causing the animals' eyes to appear luminous when a light such as that of a flashlight is directed upon them in the darkness. The tapetum functions very much like the "cat's-eye" reflectors with which we line our driveways or stake out the borders of highways. Even certain nocturnal insects have such reflective struc-

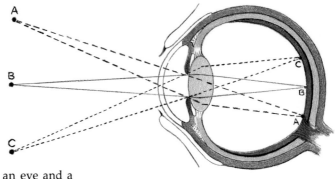

The corresponding parts of an eye and a camera. In both instances, the lens projects an inverted picture upon the background (film or retina) of each structure.

tures in their eyes, which explains why the eyes of a moth that look black in daytime will gleam in luminescent colors when caught at night in a beam of light. The eyes of such animals as cats and racoons most often show a greenish luminescence as they reflect the light of a lamp or a flashlight, and in that way lessen any blinding effect.

By and large, eyes are poorly equipped for dealing with any direct light from radiant energy sources. Although the soft, weak light of a candle or a log fire presents no difficulties, looking at the sun or any other bright light causes temporary blindness, and long exposure to strong direct light is not only very painful, but may permanently damage the eyes. As the term "snowblindness" indicates, even light that is totally reflected can have such an effect. We therefore not only shade our lamps but also reduce glare by the use of tinted sunglasses, goggles, or other devices whenever too much of the sun's light is reflected into our eyes by snow, white sand, or smooth water surfaces. Normally, however, our natural environment gives off a satisfactory and agreeable blend of the indirect, reflected light which our eyes need in order to form the images that permit us to distinguish the objects that surround us. Some of this indi-

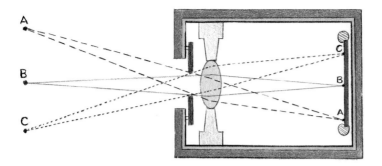

rect light, especially the blue-green light reflected by the sky
and the earth's vegetation, even has a soothing and relaxing
effect upon the optic nerves.

One might expect that the light entering through the
pupil and gathered by the lens would connect with the
light-sensitive receptor cells immediately upon reaching the
retinal area. That, however, is not the case, for the rods and
cones are located deep inside the retina and point *away*
from the eye opening and in the direction of the dark pigment "curtain" with which the back of the retina is lined.
The light therefore has to penetrate the entire thickness of
the retina before reaching the receptors. That arrangement
marks ours as an *inverse eye*, in contrast to the *converse eye* of
certain nonvertebrate animals, whose receptor cells do face
forward.

In accordance with optical laws, the light gathered by the
lens forms upon the retinal area a tiny upside-down image
of whatever the eye is looking at. Up to this point, the comparison of the eye with the camera still applies; in the case
of the camera, light entering through the lens aperture also
forms a similar small, inverted picture of the photographed
scene or object on the film in the back. From there on, however, all similarity between the camera and the eye ends.
For one thing, the camera's film has to be chemically treated
in order for the image to develop; for another, the finished
product is a permanent picture.

Needless to say, something very different occurs in the eye, which not only must produce images instantaneously, but must also continuously replace them as the eyes shift to look at different objects. Neither film nor chemical treatment is needed to produce a picture. Instead, the image formed on—or rather in—the retina is dismantled, so to speak, and then passed on in the form of impulses through the fibers of the optic nerve to the optic centers in the brain, which in humans are located well toward the back of the head. There, the dismantled "impulse image" must be put together again, turned right side up, and converted into the correct light intensities and proportions, so that we can see a life-sized, exact, and detailed image of whatever we happen to be looking at.

It should be obvious at this point that there are certain remarkable similarities between the process of seeing and that used to create television pictures, where a "light picture" is converted into electric impulses, and later reconverted back into a radiant image. As we are discovering with increasing frequency, some of the most advanced devices of modern technology resemble systems that have existed in living organisms for many millions of years. The main difference between the systems seems to be that the organic models are usually more economic as well as more refined and versatile. Only in comparison with our rather crude machines can the incredible efficiency and intricacy of living mechanisms be properly appreciated.

Take the light/impulse conversion necessary for television: it needs electrical power, a considerable amount of machinery, and crews to construct and repair it. Our visual apparatus, on the other hand, achieves a much more delicate, variable, and complex process of conversion by means of a self-contained "closed-circuit" system operating continuously, day in and day out, throughout all the waking hours of our life. Adapting itself to a variety of external con-

The brains of mammals ranging from primitive to highly organized. Areas serving the olfactory sense are shown in yellow, those serving vision, in red. From left to right: anteater, cat, primate.

ditions, our visual apparatus yields instant results, for we
*see* the moment we look, yet it does it all so smoothly that
we are never even consciously aware of it. Although both
the lens and the "screen" of our eyes are tiny, the picture
we see is life-size, and, in the normal eye, automatically
adjusted to the proper focus, intensity, and perspective. In
that fraction of a wink between looking and seeing, the tens
of millions of impulses received from the retina via the optic
nerve are processed, converted, and projected without our
even noticing it: we "simply" see. However, anyone who
has studied the eye and its functions knows that there is
nothing simple about it; despite our most advanced scientific research, we still do not fully understand the miracle of
vision.

What we do know is that eyesight becomes possible only
when all three parts of the visual apparatus—the eye itself,
the optic nerve, and the optic centers in the brain—are in
good working order and functioning correctly. Damage to
any one of them means either impairment of sight or, if the
damage is serious, complete loss of vision. Obviously, an
injury to the eye itself can render impossible the registering
of the image on the retina, which is the first vital step in the
process of seeing. But even with perfectly good eyes, there
can be no vision if the transmitter, meaning the optic nerve,
is damaged or destroyed. Finally, both the eyes *and* the optic nerve may be intact and working, but if the all-important
"computer center" in the brain does not function properly,
the impressions registered on the retina and sent to the
brain will not be converted into images, and the eyes will
remain sightless.

This means, quite simply, that we see as much or more
with our brain as with our eyes. The fact that the brain has

  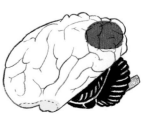

so crucial a role in eyesight explains why there can be something called "hysterical blindness," a psychological condition in which the brain fails to produce images even though there is no physical damage to any part of the visual apparatus. A person so afflicted will be blind until the psychological block is removed, whereupon sight will return.

Further proof of the extent to which we see with our brain is found in the fact that we can conjure up before our "inner eye" not only elaborate imaginary pictures, but also faithfully detailed images of objects, persons, or scenes which we may have seen days, months, or even years earlier. This huge "film library" of thousands of scenes, persons, and objects viewed by us in the course of the years is fully as astonishing as the great amount of abstract knowledge stored away in our brain. The things we see in dreams and during hallucinations are additional proof of our "inner vision," as is the ability to create mental pictures, upon which so much artistic achievement is based. Coupled with our elaborate visual memory, the mental imagery we can "dream up" must be counted among the wonders of the human mind.

Precisely because mental processes are so vital a part of vision, our knowledge of what animals see remains sharply limited and partly based upon guesswork. Despite the basic physical similarity of human eyes to those of other .vertebrates, we cannot see into an animal's mind or through its brain. Do animals have imagination? Probably not, or at least not in the human sense. But many do have visual memory, although its extent and pattern cannot be easily determined. In addition to purely anatomical research, tests designed to measure the visual faculties of animals have yielded valuable insights into what one might call the mechanical part of animal vision: visual acuity, color perception, and the ability to see in dim light. These tests have also enabled us to draw conclusions about the extent of animals' visual memory. In some instances, animals seem to recognize certain shapes, patterns, and colors more on the basis of instinct, or inherited memory, than on individually remembered experience. There is a great deal of evidence, however, that many animals learn to associate specific colors and patterns with past encounters—either pleasant or unpleasant—and behave accordingly when they see them again. Among other things, such tests indicate that birds react strongly to color patterns, whereas mammals, most of whom see little or no color, are influenced by shapes and strong contrasts. Thus a dog or a cat which has once been the victim of a skunk's "stink-bomb" attack will recognize and react to the stark black-and-white pattern of the skunk's coat, even when any chance of recognition by smell has been deliberately eliminated.

But generally, visual recognition among mammals is not of major importance, because, unlike humans, they remember scents much better than images; their acuity of smell far outranks that of sight. Everyone is familiar with the phenomenally keen noses of dogs, many of which are able to recognize and single out one particular scent from among dozens or even hundreds of others. The legendary capabilities of bloodhounds to pick up faint or partially "cold" trails is an outstanding example of the degree to which a dog can rely on its nose as an infallible guide. People have often taken advantage of that talent for their own purposes: the modern-day use of dogs to sniff out narcotics and even explosives is only one example.

Even though the eyesight of most mammals is outranked by their sense of smell—and often by hearing also—the ability to form images of their environment is still of major importance to their lives. Virtual blindness is rare—moles are among the exceptions—although rather weak eyesight is found among such widely different animals as the bat on the one hand and the rhinoceros on the other. By and large,

The eyes of browsing animals are laterally placed for a wide field of vision . . .

however, mammals have eyes that play an important part in the lives of both predators and prey. Although the size of its eyes may not tell us much about an animal's habits, their location on the head often does. For instance, the eyes of predators such as cats and wolves are invariably placed in a position that gives them good binocular vision and thus permits them to judge distances. Grazing and browsing animals—sheep, deer, and rabbits, for example—have eyes located much further back on the head and at an angle enabling them to survey a wide field on each side. Although this means reduced binocular vision, judging distances is not as important to them as watching for any suspicious movement while they are feeding.

Primates are the one group of basically nonpredaceous mammals with excellent binocular vision. Although many monkeys eat insects and small vertebrate animals, most of them, including the great apes such as the gorilla and orangutan, are vegetarians. Yet their frontally placed "predator's eyes" rank as one of the distinctive features not only

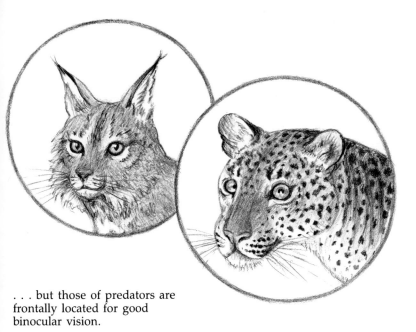

. . . but those of predators are
frontally located for good
binocular vision.

of monkeys but also of the more primitive lemurs. Another
characteristic of the primate eyesight is color vision; in contrast to most mammals, apes and monkeys seem to distinguish a range of colors identical to that perceived by
human beings.

By using their eyes to transform the environment into
shapes, movements, and scenery, vertebrate animals are
able to pursue widely varying ways of life in a world of
light. The large eyes of the gazelle and the hare with their
wide lateral field of vision serve their purpose as efficiently
as do the eyes of the cat and the fox with their ability to
judge distances and see in dim light.

For humankind, eyes that combine acuity with binocular
vision and the ability to see color have given us the chance
to utilize all our other abilities and talents, a chance that
offers vast opportunities and great challenges, and one that
is renewed for every generation.

# The Eagle's Eye

Ever since ancient times, the eagle has been one of the most favored of all animal symbols; together with the lion, it was frequently used as a royal emblem—the king of the birds and the king of the beasts. In both instances, the selection was made not entirely on the basis of the animal's strength or skill as a hunter, but also—and perhaps even more—because of its majestic appearance. There are animals that are stronger or better hunters, but there are very few that can come even close to matching the imposing dignity of the lion's maned head or the fierce-eyed regal look of the eagle. When the founders of the United States began to discuss the choice of an emblem for the new nation, there were those who favored the rattlesnake which was already emblazoned on the Revolutionary "Don't-tread-on-me" flags. Others, such as Benjamin Franklin with his down-to-earth practical sense, opted for the turkey because of its usefulness. But when the arguments were over and the votes had been counted, such considerations had gone out the window, and the regal-looking white-headed bird so inappropriately named the "bald" eagle had been chosen to represent the newly established republic.

Unlike many popular sayings, such as "wise as an owl," which has no basis in reality, the proverbial "eagle's eye" is based strictly on biological fact. The eyes of hawks, falcons, and eagles are incredibly keen, and far superior to the eyes

The kiwi is the only bird with weak eyesight. Other flightless birds, such as the ostrich, have very keen eyes.

of other birds. And that is saying a great deal, considering the fact that birds as a group have far better eyesight than any other animal. Whether they live in the jungle or on the prairie, in the mountains or along the seashore, in open woods or in dense underbrush, birds can see better than any of the creatures that share those environments with them.

In contrast to the great majority of mammals, birds have a very poor sense of smell, a deficiency that does not hamper them. They rely instead on their excellent eyesight as well as on their keen sense of hearing for success in all activities, from finding food to courting a mate to detecting potential dangers. The overwhelming superiority of their visual sense over that of smell can be convincingly demonstrated by comparing the large size of the optic lobes in a bird's brain with the small olfactory area.

The axiom that every rule has its exception applies also to the world of birds. The sole exception to the many thousands of sharp-eyed bird species is the rare and peculiar kiwi of New Zealand. Its eyesight is so weak that it must rely on its other senses for survival, especially its sense of smell, which is much better than that of all other birds. But the kiwi is atypical in other ways as well, for not only is it flightless and covered with feathers that look like hair; it also has nostrils located at the tip, rather than at the base, of its long bill, and a curious, rolling gait. Small, rather mouselike eyes and long whiskers round off the picture of a creature that hardly resembles a bird at all. Like all flightless birds, the kiwi is very vulnerable to changes in the environment. Great efforts are now being made in New Zealand to protect the kiwi and preserve its habitat of swampy forests so that it will not become extinct.

The kiwi's weak eyesight has nothing at all to do with the fact that it cannot fly. Other flightless birds have exceedingly keen vision which may rival that of some birds of prey. Both the African ostrich and the unrelated but ostrichlike South American rhea combine the typical bird's keen eyesight and poor sense of smell. That combination has led to a kind of "division of labor" between ostriches and rheas on one hand and large grazing animals such as zebras and deer on the other. By teaming up, birds and mammals can complement each others' senses. The relatively weak-eyed mammals are able to smell a predator's scent from afar, and the long-necked, sharp-eyed birds can detect any suspicious movement from great distances; the result is increased safety for both. This type of mutually beneficial partnership between two entirely different kinds of animals is known as *symbiosis,* and occurs more frequently in nature than most people realize.

With the exception of the kiwi, the only birds believed to have a better-than-average sense of smell are certain members of the vulturine group, although their keener "nose" does not come at the expense of good vision. In the past, it was assumed that all vultures must have an extremely keen sense of smell because of the speed with which they located the decaying bodies of dead animals. Later, however, increasing doubt was cast on that assumption, and some naturalists became convinced that all vultures find their food by sight alone. In an attempt to settle the argument once and for all, famed American artist-naturalist John James Audubon covered an animal carcass with canvas, and then remained in a blind nearby to see whether the cadaver would attract any vultures. The birds failed to locate it, which made him feel certain that they must be guided entirely by their eyesight while searching for food. That belief was bolstered by another test, in which an oil painting of a partially dissected sheep's carcass was used. When black vultures were attracted to the painting, there no longer seemed the slightest doubt that vision alone directed their search for carrion.

The controversy was reopened years later by Frank Chapman, another noted American naturalist. He discovered through experiment that turkey vultures could—and did—locate carcasses covered by boxes, which indicated that they must have been attracted by the odor. Further examination revealed that the olfactory area of the brain, which controls the sense of smell, is about three times as large in turkey and king vultures as in some other species such as the black vulture of California or the South American condor. Scientists seeking an explanation for that difference believe that the turkey and king vultures need a keener sense of smell because they normally frequent heavily wooded habitats. In dense underbrush, a dead—and therefore motionless—animal would be almost impossible to locate by sight alone.

The bird, or avian, eye resembles those of other verte-

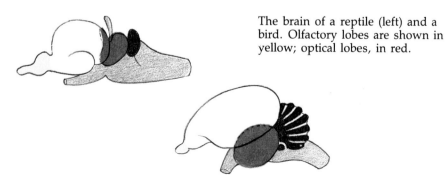

The brain of a reptile (left) and a bird. Olfactory lobes are shown in yellow; optical lobes, in red.

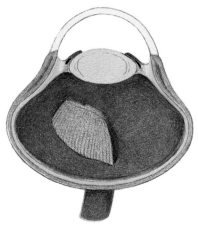

Like a miniature mountain ridge, the pecten, or comb, rises from the retinal area of a bird's eye.

*Color Code*

Cornea: yellow
Lens: blue
Iris: brown
Ligaments: tan
Iris sphincter: black
Choroid coat: green
Sclera: orange
Aqueous humor: white
Pecten: lilac
Retina/optic nerve: red

brates both in general design and structure. There are, however, some significant differences that distinguish a bird's eye from that of a mammal or an animal below the reptilian level. By the same token, certain striking similarities exist between the eye of a bird and that of a reptile such as a lizard; those similarities offer convincing proof of the close relationship that exists between the two groups.

Some of this resemblance is apparent even superficially. The eye of a chicken or a pheasant, for example, looks very much like that of an iguana or other large lizard. At a glance, and if the rest of the head is blocked out, the two sets of eyes may be all but indistinguishable. Both are surrounded by bare skin, both have lower lids that are more mobile than the upper lids, and both also have a "third eyelid" called a *nictitating membrane,* which is a thin transparent fold of skin that can be drawn across the eye beneath the other lids. In the mammalian eye, the nictitating membrane is reduced to a nonfunctional remnant in the inner corner of the eye. But birds and lizards, which have only a single, ducted tear gland, need the membrane to spread the gland's secretion evenly over the surface and also as extra protection against dehydration of the cornea.

The bird's internal eye structure also resembles the typical reptilian model in many significant details. One of the

Focus change in the reptilian and avian eye differs from that in the mammalian eye on the right. In the top half of the illustration, the muscle surrounding the iris contracts to make both cornea *and* lens more convex for near sight.

*Color Code*

Cornea: yellow
Lens: blue
Iris: brown
Ligaments: tan
Iris sphincter: black
Choroid coat: green
Sclera: orange

most peculiar and puzzling of those features is the *pecten,* or comb, which protrudes from the lower half of the retina into the vitreous humor, and is shaped somewhat like a folded concertina bellows. Although scientists are not entirely certain about the pecten's actual function or functions, they believe it to be a means by which the eye is supplied with additional blood and oxygen.

Another feature shared by both groups is the mechanism for accommodation, or focus change, which differs from that found in any other vertebrate eye. The lens of mammals, for instance, is normally adjusted for near sight, and is flattened for long-distance viewing by the action of special muscles in the choroid coat. The lens of birds and reptiles, however, is normally set for long sight, and is controlled by the ringlike muscle, or *sphincter,* which surrounds the iris. Contraction of that muscle causes the forward portions of both the lens *and* the cornea to become more convex when the bird or lizard wants to focus on nearby objects. Relaxation of the muscle returns the lens to its normal long-view focus.

Despite such marked similarities between avian and reptilian eye structures, many significant modifications within both groups reflect the differences in development and life-style that separate birds from reptiles. Snakes, nocturnal geckos, and a few other lizards lack both the outer movable eyelids and the nictitating membrane. Instead, the eye is protected by a clear, immovable "windowpane" spectacle. When snakes shed their skin, the spectacle comes away with it because a new eye covering has already formed underneath.

The majority of geckos are "cat-eyed," but in some species the inner margin of that vertical pupil is lobed, which means that, when fully closed, a row of four tiny pinholes is left to admit light into the eye. Each of these holes focuses an image on the retina, resulting in a picture that is sharper than the one formed by a single but larger pupil opening. Expressed in photographic terms, the geckos' pin-hole pupil provides a depth of focus of an f22 lens opening in light that would normally require an f4.5 aperture. Such modifications partly compensate for the lack of a fovea—the retinal area of greatest acuity—in the eyes of these lizards.

An entirely different kind of visual adaptation dis-tinguishes the true chameleons, the slow-moving lizards famed for their quick-change coloration. Their large, bulg-ing eyes are covered by thick, scaly, circular lids, which ex-pose only the pupil in the center. Accentuating their peculiar appearance is the fact that each eye can be moved independently of the other, and can be swiveled about in a complete hemisphere. That arrangement has great advan-tages, for it permits the chameleon to scan the vicinity for possible dangers with one eye, while keeping the other fixed upon some nearby insect prey. When both eyes are swiveled to a forward position, a chameleon has excellent binocular vision, and can aim the lightning thrust of its long, sticky tongue with deadly accuracy.

Keen-eyed lizards represent one extreme of the reptilian

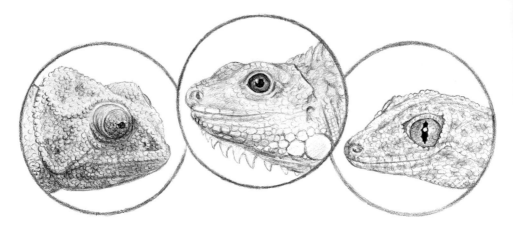

The eye of the iguana (center) is typical for many lizards. The swivel eye of the chameleon (left) and the lobed pupil of the gecko represent extremes of specialization.

scale of vision; at the other end are found the sightless or near-blind burrowers such as the worm snakes and lizards. There are no such extremes among birds, for whom good vision is the norm and phenomenally keen eyesight not unusual. Among all the vertebrate groups, birds are the only one that includes not a single blind or functionally blind species; a sightless bird is unthinkable and could not survive in the natural state.

The features that make a bird's eye so unusually keen—and that set it apart from the otherwise largely similar reptilian eye—are not revealed by the externally visible parts. Beyond the fact that a larger eye obviously admits more light than a smaller one, the size of the outer eye, or rather of the iris, is no reliable indicator of its powers. But the size of the *total* eye—meaning the eyeball—offers a very good clue because this determines the size of the retina. It comes as no surprise to find that a bird's eyeballs are proportionately larger than those of other vertebrates. They take up a considerable part of the head, and reach extremes in such species as the two-foot long snowy owl, whose eyeballs are fully as big as those of a human being.

A large eyeball provides the large retinal area needed to accommodate the great number of sensory cells, which are tightly packed together throughout the entire retina, with the exception of the raised area of the pecten. Actual counts have disclosed that the average songbird has about twice as many rods and cones per area unit as does a human being. The number may rise to as much as eight times as many for hawks, which also have two foveas instead of one. It is believed that one fovea serves the hawk's monocular vision, while the other enhances his binocular sight. The eyes of an eagle or a hawk are therefore many times as keen as those of even the most sharp-eyed human, and may be compared to the visual acuity of a person armed with a powerful pair of field glasses. Such telescopic sight explains why a hawk circling hundreds of feet above the ground can spot a mouse running through the grass below.

Birds of prey are further aided by their unusual powers of *accommodation*. In optical terms, that means an extremely rapid focus adjustment of the lens to different distances. Such speed in focus change is necessary if hawks and falcons are to zero in accurately on moving targets during

Dark markings around the eyes of the peregrine falcon reduce glare as it flies in bright light. The complete facial disk of the barn owl on the left indicates that it depends more on sound than on sight; the burrowing owl on the right hunts mainly by sight.

Birds of prey have good binocular
vision . . .

their diving flights from great heights; the so-called stoop of
the peregrine falcon has been clocked by small planes as
reaching a speed of up to 175 miles per hour.

The rule that predators must be able to judge distances
accurately applies as much to the winged eagle or falcon as
it does to the four-legged lion or bobcat. Like the eyes of
predatory mammals, the eyes of birds of prey are placed far
enough forward and at an angle that affords them good binocular vision. This is most pronounced among owls, whose
eyes are set close together near the base of the bill and
squarely facing forward.

The fruit-, seed-, and insect-eating birds, on the other
hand, need a wide field of vision while feeding. Like their
grazing and browsing counterparts among the mammals,
the nonpredatory species have eyes placed farther back on
the head and at a more lateral angle. Being able to watch
out for enemies is much more important to such birds than
is perfect binocular vision. In contrast to a bird such as an
owl, which stares squarely with both eyes at the object of its
curiosity, a robin or sparrow will cock its head and look
with one eye only at whatever it wants to see.

Hardly any binocular vision at all is possible for the
woodcock, whose eyes are placed so far back and so high

. . . but seed- and insect-eating birds need lateral vision to watch out for enemies.

that they completely fill the available space at the top of the head. Its ears, as a result, are very unusually placed below the eyes and near the base of the bill. The bird does not need its eyes to find food as it uses its long, sensitive bill to probe for worms deep below the surface of the soil. While so engaged, the woodcock would be in great danger from its enemies were it not for the fact that its large eyes afford it an exceptionally wide field of vision.

Differences in vision between diurnal and nocturnal species of birds are not so much a matter of visual acuity as of an ability to see color and bright light. The retinal cones, which are intimately connected with color perception, are most numerous in the eyes of birds active by day, and especially among the songbirds and small, flower-visiting species such as hummingbirds. Those with nocturnal habits, on the other hand, may have few or no cones at all in the retina. These include most owls and other night fliers such as whippoorwills. Their lack of color perception and reduced vision in bright light is compensated for by their greatly enhanced ability to see at night, an ability heralded by the very large size of their eyes. Actual tests have confirmed that owls need only between one-tenth and one-hundredth of the light necessary for human vision; they are able to find a dead mouse by an illumination equaling that of one standard candle placed 1,170 feet away.

Color is of little importance in the lives of these birds, which seek both their food and their mates at night, and whose courtship is vocal rather than visual. Their world is dominated by sound more than by sight, and all of them have an extremely keen sense of hearing. Owls can catch a live mouse in absolute darkness by hearing alone; their ear openings are asymmetrical and so wide apart that they can distinguish sounds coming from different directions extremely well. In addition, the characteristic flattened "facial disks" that surround the eye region are made up of small, thin, highly specialized feathers believed to be good sound conductors.

A bird that must rely on its sense of hearing, rather than on sight, in order to survive is the incredible guácharo, or oilbird, of northern South America and the island of Trinidad. Oilbirds live in the permanent darkness of seaside or mountain caves, venturing forth only at night to feed on the fruits of the oil palm. Long before dawn arrives, the birds are back in the lightless depths of their caves.

Although they have normal night vision like that of the goatsuckers and nighthawks to which they are related, eyesight could not guide the oilbirds in total darkness on their flights through the winding, twisting maze of the caverns; they would dash themselves to death against the jutting rocks. The nonvisual navigating device that guides them is a kind of built-in sonar system located in the bird's inner ear and activated by its voice. Unlike the echo-locating system of the bat, which operates on ultrasonic frequencies beyond the range of the human ear, that of the guácharo works on an audible frequency of 7,000 cycles per second. Anyone present in the caves at the time of the oilbirds' nightly flights to and from their feeding grounds can hear the deafening chorus of their screeching shrieks, groans, and screams interspersed by metallic clicking sounds that bounce off the cavern walls and so guide the birds to safety. Once they are outside the cave, oilbirds use their night vision like any other nocturnal bird to find their food sources.

But the oilbird—and indeed all nocturnal birds—represent a very small minority and are not typical of birds as a group. Of the almost 8,000 species, no more than a few hundred are active by night. The overwhelming majority of birds are creatures of light and sun and air and color, a fact that helps to explain the almost universal affection which birds have traditionally enjoyed among peoples of the world. We instinctively love the light and fear the darkness and therefore have no strong feelings of kinship for animals whose life begins at nightfall. Birds have been used as symbols of literal and figurative light since ancient times. In Egyptian mythology, Horus was the falcon-headed god of the day and the rising sun, and the falcon was his sacred animal. Thoth, the god of wisdom, was depicted as having the head of an ibis, the bird still known today as the sacred ibis. For Christians, the white dove represents the enlightenment of the Holy Ghost. Ancient myths of the fabulous phoenix picture it as rising triumphantly in rejuvenated splendor from the embers of the fire in which it sought death. In old Central American Indian cultures, the glittering quetzal was seen as the symbol and embodiment of the god Quetzalcoatl, one of the few peaceful deities known to the Aztecs. Even the cock which greets the rising sun each morning upon awakening has been used by some peoples as a symbol of enlightened wisdom. There can be no doubt that the strong affinity we feel for birds is at least partly anchored in the fact that they are such visual creatures; that for them, as for us, vision takes precedence over all other senses as they pursue their life in the world of light.

# Underwater Perspectives

Although air and water differ in many respects, the only important difference between them in the context of vision is that of optical density, or *refractive index*. That index measures the degree to which the speed and direction of light waves are affected by the density of a medium through which they have to travel. The denser the medium, the shorter the light waves, and the longer the traveling time. Because water is so much denser than air, it slows down the light considerably and at the same time deflects it from its path. Visibility is therefore greatly reduced even in still, clear water which is reasonably free from floating foreign particles. It does not take a very deep layer of water to scatter and absorb a good deal of the incoming light. At greater depths, an increasing amount of light is lost, until total darkness prevails in the ocean at less than half a mile down. The difference between seeing in air and seeing in water is enormous. It can be best appreciated by considering the detail visible on a clear day from a plane several miles up, and comparing that to the few dozen yards—at best—at which objects can still be seen clearly underwater. There cannot be any "eagle-eyed" aquatic creatures because the optical density of the medium in which they live does not permit farsightedness.

Despite that fact, every type of eye found among land animals also occurs in those that live in the water. There is

The brain of an amphibian (left) and of a fish. Olfactory lobes are shown in yellow; optical lobes, in red.

the compound eye of the aquatic arthropods such as lobsters and crabs; the simply organized eyes of marine snails; and the vertebrate's eyes of fishes and aquatic mammals. In addition, there is a fourth eye type not found on dry land: the highly organized eyes of the cephalopods—the squids and octopuses—which are developed along different lines but rival those of the vertebrates in complexity and efficiency.

Of all those eyes, only the last two are really efficient image-forming visual organs, for although both the aquatic arthropods and at least some marine snails can perceive shapes, the images they see are probably very crude. Good vision, at least by our standards, is limited to the aquatic vertebrates and the cephalopods.

Included among the vertebrates are some completely aquatic animals—primarily fish but also whales and porpoises—whose bodies are so wholly adapted to life in the water that they cannot survive long out of it. A middle ground between the totally aquatic and totally terrestrial vertebrates is occupied by those species leading what might be described as a double life. They spend their time partly in and partly out of the water, and their bodies reflect this dual standard. Although some mammals such as seals may be counted in that category, the majority is made up of the amphibians, the animal class whose very name—derived from the Greek *amphibios*—proclaims them as leading a double life.

Representing a kind of bridge between the air-breathing reptiles and the water-breathing fish, amphibians are found in or near bodies of fresh water all around the world. They never appear in the ocean because salt for them is a deadly poison. Although some species live out their entire life in the water, most are totally aquatic only during the first, fishlike larval stage of their existence and later change into air-breathing adults. Yet even these amphibians are not entirely free from the bond that ties them to the water, because as adults they must return to the water to lay their eggs; most also seek refuge in the water when escaping from their enemies.

Keenness of vision varies considerably within the amphibian group. Tiny, nonfunctional eyes distinguish the most primitive members; known as caecilians, these are legless burrowers which look like oversized earthworms. Many primitive salamanders have very weak eyesight, and some cave-dwelling species are blind as adults although they are able to see in the larval stage. As indicated by their large size, the eyes of frogs and toads are by far the keenest of all amphibians. A frog's ability to spy a flying insect and capture it in an accurately aimed jump demonstrates the acuity of his vision.

Next to their size, the most striking external feature of a frog's eyes is their prominent location atop and at opposite sides of the head. With his eyes raised well above skull level to form large globular mounds, the frog is assured a wide field of vision not only forward and sideways, but also upward and toward the rear. Although this position results in at least some reduction of binocular vision, the frog's accurate aim proves that his judgment of distance is not impaired. On the other hand, the advantage of being able to watch out for enemies on all sides is of crucial importance, for frogs are considered choice tidbits by predators from fish and snakes to birds and mammals, including human beings.

The frog's upper eyelid is just a thick fold of skin without any muscles, and therefore incapable of independent movement. The lower lid is a similar but smaller fold, which sometimes also lacks muscles. The eyeball, on the other hand, is equipped with special muscles that can pull it all the way back into its socket. When the frog swallows, the eyes are automatically retracted each time so that they press against the roof of the mouth and so help to push the food down into the gullet.

Protection of the cornea is provided by a gland connected to a tear duct, and further by a nictitating membrane that spreads the gland's secretion evenly over the surface of the eye and also safeguards the eye when the frog is underwater. Unlike those of birds and reptiles, the frog's "third eyelid" does not slide sideways across the eye but instead is pulled upward over it by tendons that encircle the eyeball. Frequently translucent rather than transparent, this third eyelid may be marbled with color patterns that vary with the species. Because of its translucence, some visual impressions are received by the eyes—and therefore by the brain—even when the frog is asleep or submerged in water, so that it is never completely off guard.

The iris of frogs and toads is often beautifully colored in gleaming gold or coppery hues that are caused by minute tissue structures reflecting portions of white light. Most frogs have horizontally oval pupils, but some that hunt at night are "cat-eyed," with vertically elliptical pupils that can be closed to a mere slit. Salamanders, which are mostly about in darkness and often spend much time in the water, have very large pupils designed to admit every bit of the available weak light.

A frog can draw a translucent third eyelid, or nictitating membrane, up across its eye to protect it, especially underwater.

In most respects, the amphibians' internal eye structure resembles that of other vertebrates. Both rods and cones are present in the retina, and the frog's color vision seems to rival that of reptiles. The most significant difference is the lack of any mechanism for accommodation. Like a box camera, the frog's eye can focus on anything within a certain range, which is believed to extend from a minimum of about three inches to a maximum of ten yards. Below the minimum, frogs cannot see objects clearly; they often back away from a potential prey, such as a worm or caterpillar, until they have put at least one full body length between them and their prospective meal, and only then snap it up.

The "double standard" which is the hallmark of amphibian life requires fundamental changes as the animals complete their metamorphosis from the fishlike larval to the terrestrial adult stage. At that time, the aquatic tadpole's eyes are transformed into those of a creature that will use its vision more in air than in water: they acquire lids, nictitating membrane, eye gland, and tear duct. Although the adult frog can still see underwater, its vision is better above the surface.

As indicated by the lack of lids and tear glands in the tadpole, these external ocular features are not needed by the wholly aquatic animals such as fish. Otherwise, however, the eyes of fish have all the usual components, including cornea, lens, and a retina equipped with both rods and cones, but the lens is spherical rather than elliptical. In water, whose refractive index is close to that of the lens substance, the spherical shape guarantees a more efficient gathering and focusing of light on the retina. As a result, however, fish are rather nearsighted, although a somewhat clearer focus for distant objects is achieved by moving the lens backward on the optical axis with the help of special retinal muscles. While the images so perceived may not be very sharp and detailed beyond a distance of a few feet, fish

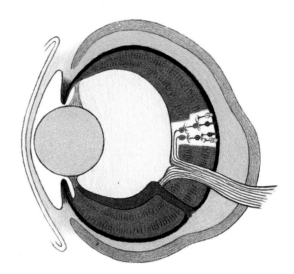

are sensitive to shadows and movements even above the water surface and can easily make out the shape of some-one moving on the river bank.

Cephalopods also have the typical aquatic animal's spher-ical lens. Although derived differently, the large eyes of a squid or an octopus are very efficient, advanced-design vi-sual organs. Their different origin accounts for the fact that theirs is a *converse* type of eye, which means that the light-sensitive cells are located in the outermost layer of the ret-ina and point toward the eye opening. Some cephalopods have a cornea, but the lens of others is directly exposed to the water. All evidence indicates that cephalopods have good vision, rivaling—and in many instances exceeding—that of the fish with which they share their environment.

The degree of visual acuity among fish covers a wide range as it does among other vertebrate groups. At the top are those species found mostly in clear water or near the surface in the ocean; these include such fast, agile predators as trout, mackerel, and barracuda. Fish living in greater depths, or in muddy, turbid waters such as estuaries, often have weak eyesight, but even keen eyes would not be of

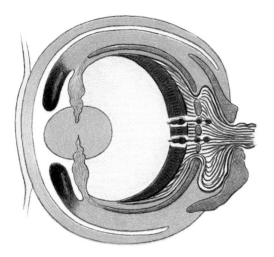

Diagram of the inverse eye of a fish (left) with its spherical lens, and the converse eye of the squid, whose light-sensitive structures face forward.

much use in such areas of reduced visibility. Other senses including smell, touch, and hearing are needed in low-visibility environments; one or all of them are highly developed among fish that either have weak eyes or live in muddy water. Catfish, for instance, can see relatively little but have the extremely sensitive, whiskerlike tactile organs that account for their name. Sharks have poor vision but their sense of smell is excellent, which accounts for the speed with which they are attracted to blood spilled in the water.

A highly developed sense of hearing is another way by which fish may compensate for their limited vision, even though their hearing is probably more a matter of sensing vibrations than of perceiving distinct sounds the way we do. Research in recent decades has revealed that the underwater environment is not the world of complete silence it once was assumed to be. Electronic listening devices have picked up, among other things, a fascinating variety of calls, whistles, squeaks, clicks, and groans made by fish communicating with one another.

What amounts to a genuine sixth sense is used by a pecu-

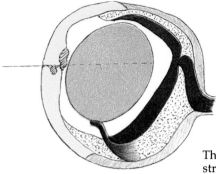

The bifocal eye of *Anableps*, the strange four-eyed fish of Central and South America. Cornea, yellow; lens, blue; retina, red; retinal muscle, purple.

liar fish living in the turbid, silt-laden waters of the Nile River, where visibility is all but zero. This eellike species sends out electric impulses to create a symmetrical electric field around its body. Any disturbance of that field by an animal swimming too close alerts the fish in much the same way a spider is warned by its keen tactile sense that an insect is struggling in its web.

An absolutely unique means of combining above-surface with underwater sight is the bifocal eye of the so-called four-eyed or periscope fish. These relatives of the minnows live in rivers and lakes in parts of tropical America where they swim about with the upper half of their bulging eyes above the surface and the other half below the water line. Divided horizontally by a membraneous band across the cornea, each eye has two pupils but only a single, bifocal lens. By keeping the upper half above water, the fish can search the surface for floating food items while at the same time watching for enemies below. The bifocal lens forms an accurate picture of each visual field on the retina. Because these fish, like all others, lack tear glands, they must constantly dip the upper eye parts in the water to keep them moist.

Because seeing in weak light requires a large lens with considerable light-gathering power, very small fish are at a disadvantage in great ocean depths; there is a limit to the size of the eyeballs that can be accommodated in a small head. The eyes of a few diminutive deep-sea species represent one solution to that problem: they have no eyeballs. Instead, a kind of tube like that of a telescope encloses the lens at one end and the retina at the other, so that the eye looks stalked. The telescope arrangement makes it possible for the fish to have a lens about five times as large as that of the eyes normally found in fish of their size. In the free-swimming species, the telescope is pointed forward, but in those that live near the ocean floor, the eye stands upright for a better view of the water above.

It might seem logical to expect that only sightless, blind creatures would choose to live in the eternal night of ocean depths into which no sunlight can reach. But nature is full of surprises, and although many blind species of fish and at least one blind squid have been discovered in the black abyss below a depth of half a mile, there are also a great many deep-sea species that can see quite well. The light which illuminates their dark world is their own, produced either by actual light organs or else by luminous bacteria which they carry with them and which are housed in special skin pouches. Although the bacteria live on the body juices of the hosts, they do not harm them in any way; on the contrary, the fish and bacteria live in a mutually beneficial symbiotic relationship. The fish supplies "bed and board," and the bacteria supply the light by which the fish can capture prey as well as recognize others of its kind.

One fish employing that method is *Photoblepharon* of Indonesia; it has large pouches filled with luminous bacteria under each eye. The strong light produced by these pouches is

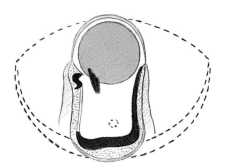

The telescope eye of *Ophistobractus*, a tiny deep-sea species. The dotted line indicates the space an eyeball with that size lens would normally occupy. Cornea, yellow; lens, blue; retina, red; retinal muscle, purple.

probably used in part to blind potential prey. Whenever the light is not needed, the fish can "turn it off" by sliding a dark membrane across the front of the pouch like a shutter.

Instead of trying to blind its prey, other luminous species may use their light as a lure. An anglerfish from two-mile ocean depths, known by the tongue-twisting name of *Galatheathauma,* makes its living with the help of such luminous bait. From the upper inside rim of its huge, cavernous mouth dangles a glowing appendage whose light illuminates that gaping maw with its rows of sharp teeth. One would think that so ominous a sight could not possibly be attractive to any potential victim, yet small fish seem incapable of resisting the lure of the light and swim right into the jaws of death. The anglerfish only has to close its mouth, swallow, and open again to have the trap set and ready for another victim.

Although the anglerfish could hardly be described as anything but ugly, some luminous deep-sea species present a beautiful sight with their rows of shining lights. One of the most attractive is the aptly named jeweled squid; it comes from the depths of the Indian Ocean and has lights of three different colors—white, blue, and red—grouped around its large eyes and on the underside of its body.

At depths much beyond two miles, luminous species begin to disappear. There seems to be in the ocean a kind of

*Photoblepharon* navigating by the light of its eye pouches filled with luminous bacteria.

The jeweled squid with its rows
of colored lights.

vertical "three-mile limit" both for the light-producing
organs and for the eyes that utilize such light. All the fish
and other marine creatures beyond that depth have no eyes
at all, or possess only small pigment spots indicating the
site where the eyes would normally be located. The sightless species of great ocean depths must rely entirely on their
other senses for guidance.

The wide range of specialized adaptations and different
lifestyles found among strictly aquatic animals, such as fish,
is not available to marine mammals that must come to the
surface to breathe. Considered objectively, the mammals
seem rather ill-suited for an underwater existence, ham-
pered by the fact that they have warm blood, must breathe
air, and bear live young which have to be suckled by the
mother. Compared to animals that can extract oxygen directly from the water, whose blood need not be heated in-
ternally, and whose young require little or no parental care,
they appear to be at a distinct disadvantage. Yet marine
mammals, from the partly aquatic seals to the fully aquatic
whales and porpoises, have successfully adapted to life in
the water, aided by such features as streamlined bodies,
heat-conserving layers of fat and blubber beneath the skin,
and air-storage compartments for deep dives.

As indicated by the varying size of their eyes, vision
among aquatic mammals ranges from fairly good to very

poor. Seals have large eyes and binocular vision like the land predators. Also like the latter, they rely heavily on their keen sense of smell, as well as on their highly developed sense of touch. Observation of some seals blinded by eye infections has proved that they can survive even without sight; several blind females observed over some length of time were able not only to feed themselves but also to raise their pups successfully.

The eyes of fully aquatic mammals are generally small in relation to their body size; some huge whales have eyes not much larger than those of a cow. Features such as movable eyelids are reminders of the fact that even whales and porpoises were originally equipped to live on land. In some deep-diving species, the cornea is very thick and hard as a protection against the enormous pressure exerted by the water on all body tissues, and the lens is set back farther in the eye. Despite such adaptations, vision among whales is generally rather weak, and they must rely more on other senses, especially on their highly developed hearing, for

Although the sperm whale is many times bigger than the giant squid, the latter has much larger eyes and keener vision.

guidance, communicating with one another through a series of eerie-sounding but often not unmusical grunts,
groans, whistles, and rumbles. Modern research, particularly that of Jacques Yves Cousteau, has thus established the factual basis of the old seamen's yarn of the
singing whale.

Except for the weak-eyed species living in the muddy waters of estuaries and rivers, porpoises have somewhat better
vision. They, too, however, depend largely upon their extremely sensitive echo-locating systems. Because water,
which impedes light, conducts sound five times as efficiently as air does, sonar navigation and communication devices are the ideal alternative to the limited vision dictated
by the optical density of water. Modern research has shown
these organic sonar systems to be infinitely more complex
and refined than even the most advanced man-made devices, which in comparison must appear clumsy and crude.

To what extent such echo-locating systems can in fact replace vision among aquatic animals has been proved by extensive experiments involving dolphins. In order to find out
whether they could locate tiny objects without being able to
see them, dolphins were blindfolded by placing small
cupped discs over their eyes and then released in a tank
strung with very thin wires and containing one small fish.
Uttering ultrasonic sounds in the range of about 100,000
vibrations per second, the dolphins made their way
through the tank without touching any of the wires and
captured the fish as surely as though they could see both
the obstacles and the prey.

The limitations imposed by water as an optical medium
prevented vision among aquatic creatures from ever becom-
ing the kind of primary sense it is for many land animals.
The degree of perfection exemplified by the eye of a bird—
or that of a human being—had to wait for life to be established on dry land.

# Color Perception

The ability to see such colors as red, green, and blue is taken for granted by most people; if they think about it at all, they accept it as a normal and commonplace part of their vision. Yet there is nothing commonplace about color perception, and despite everything we have learned about it, many of its aspects are still not well understood even today, mainly because color itself remains something of a mystery.

Ever since Sir Isaac Newton, in 1667, refuted the old belief that color was part of an object and instead proved it to be a portion of white light reflected *by* an object, scientists have tried to define and explain the nature of color. This turned out to be a difficult undertaking, however. So elusive, in fact, did color prove to be that some physicists felt impelled to deny its *objective* existence and instead relegated it to the realm of *subjective* psychological sensations. Other scientists did not agree entirely with that appraisal; today, the consensus seems to be that color should not be separated in that way because its various optical, physiological, and psychological aspects are intertwined, especially in the manner in which they affect living beings.

Color is light, and light moves forward in waves. Using something called a *diffraction grating,* a light-reflecting device produced by scratching very fine lines into a glass plate, physicists specializing in optics measured the wavelengths of white, composite light. To express the minute quantities of those wavelengths in numbers, they had to designate a special linear unit—all the existing standard units were much too coarse—called a millimicron. The length of this new unit was fixed at one millionth part of a millimeter.

Based upon this new measurement, the portion of radiant energy visible to us as light was found to reach from about 760 millimicrons for red at the extreme long-wave end to 380 millimicrons for violet at the short-wave side; beyond that extend the infrared and ultraviolet wavelengths invisible to our eye. Between red and violet are ranged all the other wavelengths, which we perceive as a band of colors or spectrum; for instance, when we see a rainbow or when we pass a beam of white light through a glass prism. Most often, however, we encounter individual wavelengths of light in the reflected colors of objects in our environment.

The knowledge that each color is light of a different wavelength led to an entirely new appraisal of color perception as the eye's ability to register, and the brain's ability to translate into specific color values, the wavelength variations that distinguish light of one color from that of another. The minuteness of these differences has to be visualized to be appreciated. When we look at a leaf reflecting light with a wavelength of 525 millimicrons, we see that light as a bright medium green. But at 475 millimicrons, the green becomes more bluish, and at 575 millimicrons, it takes on a yellowish hue. Those fifty millimicrons each way translate into only one twenty-thousandth of a millimeter, yet are sufficient for anyone with normal color vision to see as a distinctly different hue. Individuals with unusually acute color perception can distinguish between shades whose difference may be less than one hundred-thousandth of a millimeter.

The ability to see shapes and outlines, which is based

largely on the eyes' reaction to variations in light intensity, is handled mainly by the retinal rods. Seeing color, on the other hand, is a matter of registering differences in wavelengths, and seems to depend upon the presence of retinal cones. Because both processes normally occur simultaneously, one might be tempted to think that color vision is indeed just a part of general vision, were it not for the phenomenon known as colorblindness. Some individuals possess perfectly normal, image-forming vision and can see all shapes and outlines quite clearly, yet are unable to perceive color.

Colorblindness in humans is an inherited visual deficiency which affects men more often than women; the latter may pass the trait on to their children but are rarely colorblind themselves. Only about three in every one hundred persons totally lack color perception; these individuals see their surroundings as a monotone of gray shades. Partial or red/green colorblindness, however, is somewhat more common. An estimated 13–15 million people in the United States are believed to lack color perception to some degree, although many may not be aware of it until their eyes are examined. Because they see the main colors as entirely distinct shades of gray, even those individuals who are totally colorblind have no difficulty distinguishing between colors such as red and blue. Their lack of color perception can be detected only with the help of specially designed diagrams

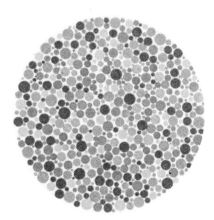

One of the diagrams used to detect colorblindness. Persons with normal color vision see a number 73 in the center; colorblind individuals cannot see the number.

and color comparisons, some of which are used widely today by the army and on drivers' tests.

The ability to understand and pinpoint colorblindness is a fairly recent development resulting from intensive studies of light and color, especially those of the past 150 years. Before that time, people knew little about colorblindness and generally assumed that all sighted creatures—humans and animals alike—saw the same range of colors. As scientists turned increasingly to the study and testing of vision and color perception in animals, many of the old assumptions were shown to be erroneous. Based upon what we know today, there seems to exist widespread color vision in every sighted animal group *below* the mammalian level. In what appears to be something of a paradox, many members of the most highly organized animal class lack the ability to translate wavelengths into colors. For instance, the widely held belief that waving a *red* flag will infuriate a bull is a misunderstanding of which factor is important. The bull sees the waving red flag as an irritating or threatening *movement* rather than as a rage-inspiring *color*. In fact, our closest domestic companions do not share our perception of color. If you have a dog or a cat, for instance, it does not see red and green and yellow the way we do, but rather—according to all available information—as grayish or perhaps brownish hues. Some zoos utilize the colorblindness of small nocturnal mammals to give visitors a chance to observe them during their nighttime activities. The cages are illuminated with red light, which the animals cannot see, thereby making them believe that they are moving in total darkness.

The only group of mammals with pronounced color vision are the primates. Because they are closer to us in physical structure than any other animal, the discovery that they share our ability to see color came as no surprise. What was surprising was the fact that, unlike both humans and lower animals, apes and monkeys seem to have very little need or use for color in their daily lives. Although some species are distinguished by brightly colored, hairless skin areas that serve as sexual signaling devices, especially in mature males, many other apes including the gorilla and chimpanzee have no outstanding coloration or markings. From what we know about their normal way of life in the wild, apes do not display even a rudimentary "artistic" interest in the colored objects of their natural environment. Yet according to the theory of gradual development, one would expect to find, in animals so close to us physically and with so highly organized a brain, some vestige of that inclination to appreciate and use color for ornamentation which was a hallmark of prehistoric men. Instead, we find this trait, not in any of the primates, but among a small group of birds that display some astonishing "artistic" talents.

Related to the birds of paradise but without their fancy plumage, the bowerbirds of Australia are noted for activities so unusual that they continue to intrigue biologists. The males of the species, as their name indicates, construct bowers that serve as courtship areas. The entrance of the finished structure is decorated with a collection of colorful ornaments; only then does the male begin to court a female and entice her into his lovenest.

One of the most accomplished of all bowerbirds is a drab-looking little fellow called the crestless gardener. First he painstakingly fashions a hutlike bower from up to 3,000 individual sticks and twigs. Then he carpets the space around the entrance with moss and finally decorates the carpet and the bower's central support with a selection of ornaments that include colorful berries, brightly patterned insect wings, and flowers which are replaced by freshly picked blossoms as soon as they fade. If a female is attracted to his decorated showplace, the male courts her while holding an orchid or other flower in his beak.

At least two species of bowerbirds decorate the walls of their bowers by painting them. They use wads of plant fibers as brushes and the juice of crushed berries as paint. One innovative male once found a half-full packet of laundry bluing and promptly proceeded to give the walls of his bower a bright blue coat of paint! The use of tools is rare enough among animals, but employing a tool for decorative purposes, rather than for a basic necessity such as getting food, is a remarkable feat for a bird.

Although bowerbirds may be unique in the way they use color perception, most birds have pronounced color vision with the exception of certain nocturnal species including night-flying owls. Because the sense of smell has hardly any part in a bird's life, color often is an important factor in the selection—or rejection—of food items. As anyone whose neighborhood is visited by orioles can readily confirm, these beautiful orange-and-black birds may be attracted to a backyard or garden by means of halved oranges fastened to a branch. Robins and other birds are noted—and notorious—for their ability to select the finest, ripest cherries, ber-

A male crestless gardener bowerbird during courtship, with an orchid in its beak.

ries, and other small fruit before people get a chance to pick them. The red/orange portion of the spectrum seems to be favored by many small birds; hummingbirds, for instance, are especially attracted by bright red flowers. For that reason, artificial hummingbird feeders are usually made of orange or red plastic, and even the commercially prepared syrup water with which the feeders are filled looks like raspberry juice.

In contrast to brightly colored fruit, brightly colored insects are usually shunned by birds which have found out from experience that such insects are almost always bad-tasting or else have poisonous stings. In much of the United States, they include the brightly patterned ladybug and milkweed beetles as well as the handsome monarch butterfly and its caterpillar, which also feeds on milkweed. Tests have confirmed that young birds quickly learn to recognize the bright "warning colors" of such insects, and after one or two attempts refuse to touch them again.

Sex recognition and courtship based upon the male's color pattern are important factors in many birds' lives. Males are often more brightly colored than females; some wear such colors all year, but others change into a special breeding plumage that replaces their duller winter dress. Still others grow long, modified plumes for use in courtship; peacocks and birds of paradise, to name only two, put on glittering, colorful performances hardly less fascinating to the human observer than to the female for which they are intended.

All available evidence indicates that color perception among the lower vertebrate groups is as widespread as among birds. Many lizards acquire brilliantly colored head-crests and dewlaps during the breeding season's courtship and combat activities. In fights between rival males, the victor's colors intensify but those of the loser quickly fade. An outsider can tell the outcome of the contest by the colors of the combatants: a defeated and therefore pale-colored male will make no further moves toward the female.

With the exception of certain newts, amphibians do not seem to make much use of color during mating season; courtship among frogs, for example, is mostly vocal. Many male fish, on the other hand, are much like birds in that they change their color patterns in the breeding season and then take great pains to display their finery so that the female can properly see and appreciate them. Acceptance of a male by a female appears to be based largely on visual approval in such species. Contests among male fish are common and sometimes hard-fought. As among lizards, the outcome of the battle is often signaled by the loser's paling colors as he yields to the victor and leaves the battleground.

Many fish rely at least partly on their color vision as a guide in selecting food items. Anyone who uses the various artificial lures and flies in fishing knows that color can be an important factor in attracting the fish. Some fish are very discriminating and will be interested only in fairly good imitations of real bait animals. Others, including bass, often seem ready to snap at any brightly colored or shining lure even if it has little or no resemblance to any living prey.

Certain small fish with bright color patterns depend on the color perception of other species rather than their own. Their survival rests on the ability of other, larger fish to recognize them by the colored "uniforms" they wear which identify them as partners in a very unusual relationship known as "cleaning symbiosis." The small fish are the cleaners and the larger ones the clients in a mutually beneficial association, whereby the smaller partners feed on the parasites, fungus growths, and diseased tissue of the larger fish. So popular is this service that there exist regular "cleaning stations" in some parts of the ocean where client fish line up and patiently wait their turn.

Two fishing lures. On the left, a streamer fly used for trout and landlocked salmon; on the right, a Bunyan fly and spinner also used for freshwater game fish.

At first glance, the cleaners seem to be engaged in the kind of work whose perils far outweigh any possible benefits. Swimming and poking around in the open mouth of a predator who normally considers any smaller fish a tasty snack appears to be a high-risk job. But appearances are deceptive, for in hundreds of observations not a single instance has been reported of a client fish attacking or eating one of the cleaners. There can be no doubt that the cleaners' immunity is based upon recognition by the larger partners of the distinctive "uniform" they wear, which in practically all species consists of brightly colored lateral stripes on a contrasting background. The few known kinds of cleaner crabs and shrimps are similarly patterned in bright colors, the boxer shrimp being elegantly banded with crimson red on a snow-white body.

Every observation and experiment designed to test color perception in animals indicates that all vertebrates capable of perceiving color, from primates to fish, see the same range of colors that make up our visible spectrum. Whether or not they experience color sensations that are identical to ours is another matter, for no human can see through the eyes of a bird or a fish. Yet it would appear that they do

Although these two small fish are entirely different species, they both wear the striped "uniform" of contrasting colors that marks them as cleaners.

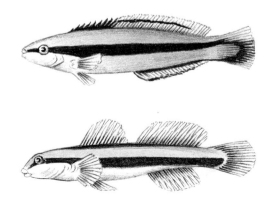

perceive these colors very much the same way as we do, and the same is true also of certain invertebrate animals. Squids and octopuses, for instance, seem to have our color range, and so do certain arthropods. Tests with butterflies indicate that they—but not night-flying moths—see much the same colors we perceive, as do the most visually oriented of all insects, the dragonflies. Experiments have shown that male dragonflies, when confronted with a number of artificial female models, will react only to those models that have the color pattern of the female. Many other details do not seem to matter much—they will, for instance, accept a model with five wings or only three—but any difference in color pattern immediately excludes the model from consideration as a potential mate. Damselflies, the smaller members of the group, display the same keen color appreciation and sometimes are attracted to the brightly colored paint spots on the floats of fishing lines. Colored bands, spots, and patches on the bodies and wings of male damselflies have an important part in sex recognition and in contests between rival males. In threat displays designed to warn off any intruder, a male damselfly will raise and expose the brightly colored tip of its abdomen. Researchers who painted the tip a different color all but eliminated a

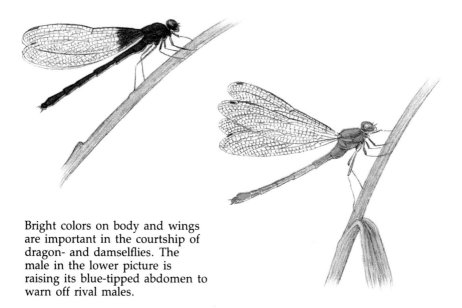

Bright colors on body and wings are important in the courtship of dragon- and damselflies. The male in the lower picture is raising its blue-tipped abdomen to warn off rival males.

male damselfly's chance of winning a mate and defending his territory. The keenness of these insects' color vision is perhaps best demonstrated by the actions of one species, whose males have brightly colored legs. In courting a female, the male flies back and forth in front of her and dangles his colorful legs before her eyes. Presumably, the male with the most attractive legs wins the bride.

The most extensive tests of color perception among insects were part of Dr. von Frisch's decades-long studies of honeybees. They yielded a treasure trove of new information, especially about the connection between the color vision of the pollinating insects and the colors of the flowers that are serviced by them. That such a connection did exist was taken for granted; the difference between the usually small, inconspicuous greenish or brownish flowers of most wind-pollinated plants, and the much bigger and often showy, colored blossoms of those pollinated by insects had long been noted by naturalists. Not known was the extent to which flower colors, rather than scents, attract the bees, or whether the colors they see match those which we perceive. Dr. von Frisch set out to gather evidence that would provide answers to both questions.

The project was not a simple one; every fact had to be established by long and painstaking experiments. Confirming previous observations that bees can distinguish between such colors as red and blue was relatively simple. All it required were three pieces of paper of the same size, two of them colored blue and one red, and a few drops of honey. One of the blue papers with the honey on it was placed on a table out in the open. The bees soon were attracted to it and so were trained to feed from that blue paper. Then that paper was removed and replaced with the empty blue square; at the same time, the red paper was placed next to it so that the bees now had two squares to choose from. When they returned, they unhesitatingly settled on the blue paper, thereby proving that they not only remembered the color but could distinguish it from the red.

Interesting as that test was, it did not offer proof that bees can see *color*. It was theoretically possible that they made their selection in the same way a colorblind person can tell blue from red: because they look like two very different shades of gray, one light, one dark.

For the main series of tests, Dr. von Frisch therefore devised a foolproof way of establishing whether his bees were indeed seeing the *color* of the squares, or just their degree of brightness. He and his researchers used a kind of checkerboard made up of many pieces of paper ranging from almost white to all shades of gray to nearly black. A single blue square was placed among the many gray ones. Small glass dishes were then set out on each of the squares. All except the one on the blue paper were empty, and that one dish contained a few drops of sugar water, which had been substituted for honey to exclude any possibility that scent might play a role in the bees' choice.

Soon the bees arrived, found the dish with the sugar water, and began to feed. Whenever they left with one load, the blue square was moved to a different position on the board in their absence. But regardless of where it was located, they headed straight for it each time on their return and ignored the gray squares. Here, then, was clear proof that bees see blue as a *color* and distinct from any shade of gray.

The test worked equally well with yellow, but when a bright crimson-red paper was used, it failed. Bees trained to feed on a red paper alone could not quickly locate it again when it was placed among the gray squares on the checkerboard and settled on many of the dark gray or nearly black papers before finally finding the red square with the sugar water. That test seemed to prove beyond any doubt that bees are red-blind, meaning that crimson, fiery red shades are to them indistinguishable from dark gray. But when a bluish-red or purplish color was substituted for the crimson shade, they located it without difficulty.

In the next series of tests, bees were first trained to feed from single, brightly hued squares with such colors as orange, green, and violet; each training square was then placed in another checkerboard, this time one made up of a variety of other bright hues. To the surprise of the observers, bees showed themselves incapable of distinguishing between many colors that to us look very different indeed. Trained on a yellow square, for example, they confused it with orange and greenish-yellow papers on the checkerboard. Similarly, those trained on a blue square would try the mauve, lilac, and purple papers as often as the blue one. Yet blue-green was different; a bee trained to find food on such a square never confused it with any other shade of either blue or green.

Adding the results of his tests to the previously established fact that bees can see ultraviolet light, Dr. von Frisch was ready to designate the range of their color vision. The biggest difference between their spectrum and ours is the shift toward the short-wave end; it lacks red but reaches over yellow, blue-green, and blue all the way to ultraviolet.

The fact that ultraviolet is an important color to bees also helped to solve an apparent contradiction between their preference for many white flowers and their indifference to white training squares. Optical examinations of white flowers disclosed that they absorb ultraviolet light and that bees therefore would see the flowers, not as white, but rather as blue-green.

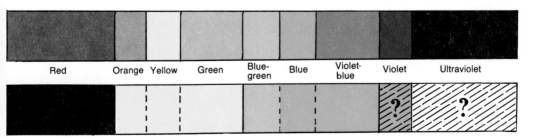

At the top, the human color spectrum.
Below, the colors of the bee's spectrum.

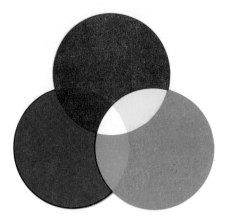

Diagram of the trichromatic theory of light. Where two primaries overlap, complementary colors are created; the overlap of all three in the center results in white light.

For a better understanding of that conclusion, the basic principles of what is known as the *trichromatic theory of light* must be considered. The theory assumes that what we see as "white" or colorless light is actually made up of three main color sensations and that all other colors are simply mixtures of any two of those three. For humans, the three colors are red, green, and violet-blue; they are called *primaries*. Wherever two of those primaries overlap, mixed colors are formed. Red and green make yellow; green and violet-blue make "cold" blue, and red and violet-blue make the pinkish-red shade called magenta. The mixed colors are known as *complementaries*, because the addition of any one of them to the remaining primary will complement, or complete, the trio of colors needed to make white light.

The complementary principle also works in reverse: filter a primary out of white light, and the remainder takes on the color of the complementary: a yellow flower absorbs violet-blue light and reflects the red and green light which combines to make the color we see as yellow.

Based upon the tricolor theory, any white flower that absorbs ultraviolet light, which is one of the bee's primaries, would reflect both yellow and blue light, and would therefore look blue-green to the bee. We have no idea what the two remaining complementaries of the bee's spectrum look like, for both are mixed with ultraviolet, which we humans cannot see. We can now, however, measure this reflected ultraviolet light by the use of a spectroscope.

In view of such discoveries, the most common colors of wildflowers take on a special significance in regions where bees are the main pollinators. White, blue, yellow, and pinkish shades abound throughout the temperate zones; all of them look as attractive to the bees as they do to us, even though they see at least some of them differently. To them, an apple orchard in full bloom is not a mass of snowy blossoms interspersed with light green leaves, but rather a mass of bright blue-green stars set off against some pale yellowish-gray foliage. Where we see a meadow with white daisies, red clover, blue chicory and yellow buttercups in green grass, they see pale yellowish grass dotted with blue-green, blue, and yellow shapes, all of them welcome signs for the winged observers.

Proving the theory that bees are red-blind did run into a few obstacles at first. The many wild-growing red flowers of tropical regions presented no problem, for those flowers are mostly pollinated by small birds such as nectareaters and hummingbirds. All but one of the relatively few bright red flowers of temperate regions could be dismissed because they are visited by butterflies, which do see red. But the large, showy red poppy of Eurasia was another matter, for poppies, which grow wild in fields and along roadsides, are eagerly sought by bees. That seemed to upset the theory about their vision, for they would not seek out a flower which to them was an unattractive shade of dark gray. For a while, the poppy was the main obstacle to accepting the findings about the bees' color perception until the problem was solved by a spectroscopic examination of the flower. The results of that test showed that the poppy reflects not only the red light which we see, but also the ultraviolet which we cannot see, but which is such an attractive color to the bees. To them, the red poppy gleams in shades of the mysterious "bees' purple" which must forever remain not

The colors of wild flowers as a human sees them . . .

. . . and as a bee might well perceive them.

only invisible but indeed unimaginable to us.

Even a brief survey of the role of color perception in the lives of different animals will convey some idea of its importance to many areas of their existence. For most animals, it serves as a kind of language or interpretation of signals in situations ranging from sex recognition to food selection. For human beings, color vision is not necessary to success or survival in any of those areas, even though it may heighten their enjoyment in all of them. But colorblind people experience physical attraction and enjoy food just as the rest of us do, even though they can't see any colors. There is no reason to believe that human beings could not live and survive without any color perception at all although, of course, vision itself is essential to human survival.

But simply surviving has never been enough for human beings. We have always sought more. From the very beginning, our color vision has been used mainly for activities that went beyond the satisfaction of mere material needs. Our history—and most certainly our cultures—would have been significantly different without the many areas of human activity made possible only by our color perception. As we admire a painting, read a well-printed book with colored illustrations, or decorate our homes with colorful furnishings, we derive aesthetic satisfaction and pleasure through our ability to see color. The same holds true for our natural environment; whether we look at the beauty of a flowering garden, watch a colorful bird, behold a flaming sunset or a fall landscape with its fiery red and gold tones, or even the many subtly different green shades of a summer scene, color perception gives us a heightened sense of living. If ordinary vision was the prerequisite for humankind's progress, color vision was the special gift, the bonus without which much of the beauty of our world would remain invisible to us.

# Index